CASE STUDIES IN
CULTURAL ANTHROPOLOGY

GENERAL EDITORS
George and Louise Spindler
STANFORD UNIVERSITY

THE HIGHLAND CHONTAL

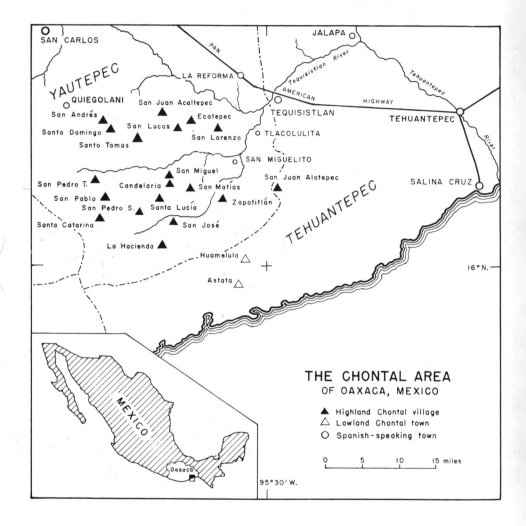

SAN CARLOS

JALAPA

YAUTEPEC

QUIEGOLANI

San Juan Acaltepec

LA REFORMA

PAN

Tequisistlan River

Tehuantepec

San Andrés

Ecatepec

AMERICAN

HIGHWAY

TEQUISISTLAN

TEHUANTEPEC

Santo Domingo

San Lucas

San Lorenzo

TLACOLULITA

Santo Tomas

SAN MIGUELITO

River

San Miguel

San Juan Alotepec

SALINA CRUZ

San Pedro T.

Candelaria

San Matias

San Pablo

Zapotitlán

TEHUANTEPEC

San Pedro S.

Santa Lucía

Santa Catarina

San José

16°N.

La Hacienda

Huamelula

Astata

MEXICO

Oaxaca

95°30'W.

THE CHONTAL AREA
OF OAXACA, MEXICO

▲ Highland Chontal village
△ Lowland Chontal town
○ Spanish-speaking town

0   5   10   15 miles

THE HIGHLAND CHONTAL

By
PAUL R. TURNER
University of Arizona

HOLT, RINEHART AND WINSTON, INC.

NEW YORK   CHICAGO   SAN FRANCISCO   ATLANTA
DALLAS   MONTREAL   TORONTO   LONDON   SYDNEY

Cover photograph: *A native curer setting fire to copal (a tree resin) upon which he has placed a raw egg. If the egg explodes, the ritual is believed to be effective.*

Library of Congress Catalog Card Number: 77-178592
ISBN: 0-03-086267-1
Printed in the United States of America
2 3 4 5 6   059   1 2 3 4 5 6 7 8 9

*To BILL KELLY who encouraged me to become visible
in these pages*

Foreword

About the Series

These case studies in cultural anthropology are designed to bring to students, in beginning and intermediate courses in the social sciences, insights into the richness and complexity of human life as it is lived in different ways and in different places. They are written by men and women who have lived in the societies they write about and who are professionally trained as observers and interpreters of human behavior. The authors are also teachers, and in writing their books they have kept the students who will read them foremost in their minds. It is our belief that when an understanding of ways of life very different from one's own is gained, abstractions and generalizations about social structure, cultural values, subsistence techniques, and the other universal categories of human social behavior become meaningful.

About the Author

Paul R. Turner is Associate Professor of Anthropology at the University of Arizona. He has previously taught at the University of Nebraska, the University of Oklahoma, and Wheaton College. He did his graduate work at the University of Chicago and received his M.A. degree in 1964 and his Ph.D. in 1966. His fieldwork was done among the Highland Chontal Indians while he was a linguistic missionary with the Summer Institute of Linguistics from 1959–1963. At present he teaches anthropological linguistics and introductory anthropology. His publications to date include articles that have been published in applied anthropology and linguistic journals.

About the Book

This case study of the Highland Chontal is a direct and personal account of another culture. The author uses practically no jargon and takes the stance of an American telling other Americans "how it is" with the Chontal. He explains how the reader might react to the situation being described. The author's own involvement as a missionary and a human being, which takes over dramatically in the last couple of pages, is somehow present throughout the whole treatment. The case study has an especially sincere and honest quality.

The Highland Chontal is not intended primarily as a contribution to

Middle American studies, although there is some new cultural information contained in it. The student reader, however, will be less concerned with this contribution than with the simple, clear, and direct understanding it provides of another way of life in a land very close to our own, which has assumed increasing significance in recent years.

Some notable features of the case study include an excellent account of the Chontal kinship system laid out in a modern componential manner and explicitly compared to that of the United States. It is made particularly meaningful by relating social behavior and attitudes to kinship terms. There is also a very good account of socialization, in both its familial and community dimensions, and of magically caused illness and curing.

The book is clearly and effectively organized in terms of soical, cultural, and personality systems. The section on cultural change provides a useful perspective on the implications of purposeful cultural change by cultural agents of a different cultural system from that of the people whose behavior is being changed. Best of all this chapter shows how experience in other cultures affects the observer so that he returns to his own culture a different person from when he began his fieldwork.

George and Louise Spindler
General Editors

Phlox, Wisconsin

Acknowledgments

The field work that produced the data for this book can be divided into two periods: 1959–1963 and 1964–1969. During the first period I was associated with the Summer Institute of Linguistics and lived with my wife and daughter in the village of the San Matías Petacaltepec. During the second period I was a graduate student and, later, a professor of anthropology. I made yearly visits to San Matías that lasted from two weeks to two months. These trips were supported by grants from the American Philosophical Society, the Doris Duke Foundation, a University of Nebraska Research Grant, and a University of Arizona Research Grant. These agencies made it possible for me to continue my study of the Highland Chontals and I want to express my appreciation to them for their help.

Viola Waterhouse introduced us to the Highland Chontals and shared her impressive knowledge of them with us. I am indebted to her in ways too numerous to mention.

I want to thank the Mexican government for the privilege of living in Mexico. In particular, the villagers of San Matías deserve mention because they allowed me to study their culture even though this involved adjustments for both them and us.

What I know of anthropology was taught to me by my teachers at the University of Chicago and they deserve the credit for whatever is good in this book.

Appreciation is due to Mr. Edwin N. Ferdon, Jr., who made the map of the Chontal area.

Finally, as I mentioned earlier, my wife and daughter shared the experience with me of living in a Mexican Indian village. They both directly and indirectly had a part in writing this book. They helped me collect the data in some instances, and also made it possible for me to be a participant-observer of these people for an extended period of time under less than ideal living conditions. Also, my wife deserves recognition as critic and typist of the final draft.

Paul R. Turner

Contents

CASE STUDIES IN
CULTURAL ANTHROPOLOGY

GENERAL EDITORS
George and Louise Spindler
STANFORD UNIVERSITY

THE HIGHLAND CHONTAL

Introduction

THE CHONTAL INDIANS of Oaxaca are one of the least known Indian groups in Mexico today. This statement can be supported by a search at any library in the United States for references about them (there are few) or by trying to find a description of them in an encyclopedia (there is none). The history of these Indians is also complicated by the fact that the name "Chontal" was given by the Aztecs to several linguistically separate groups of Indians who did not speak Aztec, stretching from the state of Guerrero, Mexico, to Nicaragua. Both historians and linguists have made serious mistakes by not realizing that the name applies to separate tribes of Indians.

To avoid some of this confusion, the name "Tequistlateco" has been used in the literature to refer to the Oaxaca Chontals. There are, however, two Oaxaca Chontal languages: one spoken by a mountain group and the other by a coastal group. The two languages are obviously related but mutually unintelligible and the cultures are contrastive as well. Because of these very real differences between the two groups I have used the name "Highland Chontal" to refer to the mountain people in general and the people of San Matías in particular.

The conceptual scheme used in this book involves an attempt to integrate the static structural–functional approach of social anthropologists with the dynamics of cultural change. Chapters 2–4 emphasize the structural-functional aspects of the society by considering it to be an organic whole composed of systems and subsystems. The terms "systems" and "subsystems" are used to indicate that the various aspects or parts of the Chontal society are interrelated and have implications for each other. An attempt is made to trace these interrelationships in terms of three main systems: the social, cultural, and personality systems. The emphasis in these chapters is on the equilibrium that is present in this society and in any society that continues to exist. Chapters 1 and 5 emphasize the basis and nature of the tensions that are inherent in the society as well as those that are a result of the larger context of the Mexican society in which it must function.

1

Dysfunctional characteristics of the Highland Chontal society will be mentioned, at times, which may sound like biased or ethnocentric opinions. These statements should be interpreted not as value judgments, but as part of developing the overall conceptual scheme mentioned above which requires treating both the functional and dysfunctional aspects of the culture of these people as they are part of a larger society.

The use of the first person pronouns "I" or "we" (including my family) rather than a more oblique third person reference occurs quite often in this book. This is meant to emphasize the interaction between these mountain people and myself as a participant–observer of their culture. I affected them and they affected me; this book is the result of that interaction.

1

Background

THE HIGHLAND CHONTALS are one of the more isolated groups in Mexico today. This does not mean to imply that they, or any other group in Mexico, are a self-contained society without important relationships to an outside world. These relationships must be taken into account in describing their culture or a serious misrepresentation will result. In fact, much of their behavior can only be understood by looking at it with these larger spheres of influence in mind. They are a source of tension and a factor for change in the life of every one of these individuals. The rest of this chapter will describe and trace out the ties that link a Highland Chontal to his nation, state, district, region, and village.

National Relationships

The Chontals (Highland and Lowland) may have been subjugated at least twice in their history. The first subjugation that we have any evidence of was by the Aztecs, and this evidence is only inferential since there is no written or oral record of such a conquest. The inferential evidence consists of about a half dozen nouns in the Chontal language that appear to have been borrowed from Aztec sources. It is possible, of course, that borrowing took place without conquest. However, this does not appear to be the case with the Chontals who are surrounded by dialects of Zapotec and yet have not borrowed any of their words. A Zapotecan group did drive the Chontals out of the Miahuatlán area of the state of Oaxaca but neither they, nor any other Zapotecans, were able to effectively subjugate the Chontals.

The Spaniards were the next conquerors of the Chontals and by that time they were settled in their villages in both the highland and the lowland areas. The lowland villages were taxed earlier and heavier than the mountain villages, which were more difficult to bring under control. The Dominican friars were mainly responsible for making contact with the mountain people at that time and exposing them to some of the beliefs of Christianity and Spanish culture. There are reports to the effect that by the end of the seventeenth century the Chontals were known as far as the state capital as a prosperous people who owned horses and dressed in fine silks. No mention is made of their source of wealth but there is speculation that it came either from selling crops (or a crop product) or raising cochineal bugs that were sold for making dye. If it were the first alternative, then there must have been a greater rainfall at this earlier time—a fact supported by oral history. If the second alternative were true, then the market must have drastically changed by the next century, because, whatever their source of wealth was, it disappeared, as well as any further mention of the Chontals. The Chontals remained in obscurity until nineteenth century linguists began classifying the languages of Mexico.

The present-day ties that the Highland Chontals have to the nation of Mexico are rather weak. They themselves classify all nonspeakers of Chontal as foreigners; that includes Spanish speaking Mexicans as well as Americans. Part of the confusion in the minds of many of these mountain people is that they think in terms of a village being the largest political unit and so they ask a person what village he comes from when they want to identify him. The confusion is compounded for them on a national level because both the capital city and the nation have the same name: Mexico. On an international level some of the more bilingual ones may find it confusing that the names for Mexico and America both begin with "Estados Unidos. . . ."

The national government affects the lives of these people in a variety of ways, but the two most important ones are probably the antimalarial campaign, which has all but eradicated malaria, and the allocation of federal school teachers whose salaries are paid by the government. These school teachers have succeeded in teaching children how to read Spanish even though for many of them it is not the language spoken in their homes. The school teachers have been the most important cultural change agents in the lives not only of the children but also of the adults. One teacher, for example, is responsible for showing people how to bake bread in San Matías. Perhaps the best way to measure their effectiveness as agents of change would be to compare the quality and quantity of Spanish spoken in those villages that have had one or more school teachers over a period of years with those that have not. Not only do the children and adults use more and better Spanish in those villages that have had permanent school teachers, but the same villages are also more receptive to other forms of cultural change.

State Relationships

The seat of the state government is in Oaxaca City, where the mountain people pay their taxes on the production of mescal, a whiskey-like drink made from the maguey plant. Oaxaca is also the residence of their state representative. He is responsible in part for supplying the villages with school teachers and helping them with intervillage land disputes. Besides the trips of village officials to Oaxaca, some of the more enterprising individuals also go there to buy merchandise to sell in their stores or for their own personal use. The trip costs about twenty-five pesos (or two dollars) round trip by bus from the Pan-American highway. Tehuantepec is closer, but the lack of certain items there, plus the the greater variety of goods and the cheaper prices in Oaxaca, make it worthwhile for some to make the longer trip. The trip from San Matías involves a day's walk to the highway and then a six or seven hour bus ride to cover a distance of about 100 air miles. Less than 10 percent of the adults in San Matías have ever been to Oaxaca and that includes only two or three women. The following account describes the impression of a man from San Matías in his forties who went to Oaxaca with me for his first visit:

> We looked around in Oaxaca. We bought the things that we wanted. We bought our food to eat. And we bought the things that other people in the village had asked me to buy for them. We brought back cigarettes and water jars. Oh, we also bought some notebooks. We brought back a harmonica. Then we came back to Mitla.
>
> Tomorrow I will be on my way. I'm going back to my village. I will get on the bus and ride it to Tequisistlán. When I get there, I will begin walking home. I will cross the river back and forth until I climb up to my village. When I get there I will say, 'It is really beautiful where I went. I saw what the village of Mitla is like as well as Tlacolula and Oaxaca. They are big, beautiful cities. They have big buildings. They have lots of clothing and fruit for sale. In Oaxaca you can buy whatever you want to eat. It has everything. Life is really enjoyable there.'

He did not mention in this account the shabby treatment he and every Indian receives from those Mexicans who consider themselves to be superior. He could have told about the clerk in the hat store who discouraged him from trying on any hats and only reluctantly sold him one. Another Indian who went to Oaxaca with me had difficulty getting waited on in one store and mistook a customer for the clerk and asked him about some merchandise. The customer refused to even acknowledge the Indian's question. When we went to eat in a second-class hotel, the waiter spotted him as an Indian and picked on him for one minor breach of etiquette after another during the entire meal. I wondered what kind of treatment he would have received in that hotel if he had been by himself, but of course he would never have put himself in such an embarrassing situation if he had any choice. Oaxaca is a big city for these Indians to visit and they enjoy it for a while, but cultural differences and class prejudice soon convince them that they do not belong.

There are very few mountain people living in Oaxaca. Besides the former state representative who comes from the village of Ecatepec, there is a younger man whom I know who fled to Oaxaca to escape prosecution as a murderer (1955) and works as a laborer. He visits his village of San Matías every year or so and could come back to live permanently, but he evidently has been able to make the adjustment and prefers to live near Oaxaca.

Tehuantepec is important to the highland people as a market and fiesta city that some might visit once or twice in a year. There are a few who live there permanently but they are the laborers and poorer people who are definitely on the fringes of the Zapotec-dominated city.

Salina Cruz should be mentioned because of the rather large mountain population that has settled in and near this city. These people have left the highlands for what they thought was a better opportunity to make a living. Many of them continue to raise crops, but some of the younger males have been able to learn other skills, such as baking bread, and are becoming an integral part of the community.

A number of mountain people have also settled in and around La Reforma and Tequisistlán, towns on or near the Pan-American highway. In both instances they are either hired laborers or they farm pieces of land.

The mescal that is made in San Matías and nearby towns is taken down to Huamelula and sold there. This town and Astata are the two main villages of the Lowland Chontal, which number about 5000 people. Highland people also visit these villages during their annual fiestas but few Lowland Chontals ever visit the highland villages at fiesta time or any other time. There are a few mountain people living in lowland villages but no lowland people live in the mountain area. The languages of the two groups have changed so much from a common origin that they prefer to use Spanish rather than their own languages in conversing with each other. Actually the lowland people are either completely bilingual or cannot speak the Lowland Chontal language. The situation is reversed among the mountain people who are bilingual to a limited extent or cannot speak Spanish at all.

District Relationships

The Highland Chontals live in the district of Yautepec which is governed by the village of San Carlos Yautepec, about two days' walk from the mountain villages. There each year the newly elected president of San Matías goes to inform the officials of his election. There also is where individuals from San Matías go when they feel that they cannot get justice in their own village. A decision from San Carlos carries a great deal of weight; it is backed up by officials who can and do sentence people to heavy fines and lengthy jail confinements. Heavy fines are seldom meted out in any of the mountain villages and no one is ever jailed for more than a few days so that people have an understandable respect and even fear of San Carlos justice. This may be the reason why few people ever take their cases to San Carlos, and when they do, only one of the parties involved makes the trip. The judgments are in favor of the party who presents his case, and probably rightly so, since he would only make the trip if he sincerely believed that he had been wronged. Cases that I know of involving people from San Matías that have been referred to San Carlos deal with murder (1955, 1966), cattle thievery (1955), land disputes (1962), property damage (1962), and religious persecution (1967).

Regional Relationships

There are nineteen mountain villages that can be considered to be Highland Chontal either because the majority of their people still speak this language or, as in the case of Ecatepec, it is the closest administrative center. The combined population of these villages is somewhere near 7500 people.

The highland area is about one day's travel by horseback from the Pan-American highway and each village in turn is no more than one day's travel by mountain trail from any other village. The most important topographical feature of the area is a branching river. The northern branch is impassable at times during the rainy season with only a suspension bridge allowing men on foot to cross. With few exceptions, to cross either branch of the river involves a descent of one to three hours and an ascent of a comparable distance at a much slower rate. Both branches of the river merge east of San Matías into the Tequisistlán river.

The villages on the northernmost ridge tend to be higher in elevation than the other villages. The highest village on this ridge, Santo Tomás, is about 8000 feet above sea level. The other villages on this ridge are about 1000 feet lower except for San Lorenzo which is around 6000 feet in elevation. The villages located between the branching river go from about 6500 feet (San Pedro S.) northeastward to 5000 feet (San Matías) and northwestward to about 5500 feet (San Pedro T.). The villages south of the southern branch of the river go from about 5500 feet (Zapotitlán) to perhaps 4000 feet (San José) and have the most dependable source of rainfall of any of the villages in this area.

The mountain villages can be ranked in terms of importance on the basis of their populations and wealth. There would be some uncertainty about the towns that rank in the center but little doubt about the towns at either end of the scale. Ecatepec is clearly the most important highland village, and at one time in the past was the head of one of the divisions of the state of Oaxaca. Ecatepec is not so much larger (it has 200 houses) than the other villages, but its people are the wealthiest people in the area. They have made their money by producing mescal, selling goods, and teaching school. As was mentioned earlier, the former state representative for the Highland Chontals is from Ecatepec. He is undoubtedly the most politically influential Chontal to have ever lived in one of these mountain villages. There are six federal school teachers employed in Ecatepec, twice as many as are working in any other mountain village. Some of the school teachers employed in the other mountain villages are natives of Ecatepec being supported by either the federal government or the village in which they teach. Ecatepec has a telegraph office connecting it with San Carlos. It also has the main post office for the area as well as being the head of the school district for the mountain villages. Chontal is spoken by only a few of the older people in Ecatepec and none of the younger generation are fluent or even interested in learning this language.

There is some uncertainty as to the next most important village in the area. San Pedro T. has more houses than Zapotitlán (150 versus 100) but may not have as many wealthy people. Both villages lie on the periphery of the area and their influence is not as great as it would be if they were more centrally located or had administrative importance.

The three smallest villages are San Andrés (nine houses), San Pedro S. (twenty-five houses), and San Lucas (thirty houses). Two of these three villages, San Andrés and San Lucas, are satellite in nature to the larger villages of Santo Domingo and Ecatepec respectively.

There are two villages, La Hacienda and Santa Catarina, that I have never visited. Their location on the map of the Chontal area is only meant to be an approximation. Half of the people of San José left their village a number of years before we arrived and formed the new village of La Hacienda about a day's distance to the south. The village of Santa Catarina used to be located between Santa Lucía and San Pedro S. The constant friction over land was the main reason why the people of Santa Catarina moved about a day's travel to the west. Both La Hacienda and Santa Catarina are so far from the other highland villages that they have little or no influence on them.

The rest of the villages fall somewhere in-between the extremes mentioned above with San Miguel outranking San Matías, the focus of this study. San Miguel is mentioned specifically because of an incident that happened soon after our arrival in San Matías and which illustrates the interrelationships that exist between each one of these mountain villages. We suggested to the people of San Matías that we would be interested in having an airstrip built for a small plane which would provide transportation and supplies for us as well as emergency service for them. They never understood from the beginning the full implications of the amount of work involved in such a project or the very limited and indirect benefits that they would receive, but they started to work on a suitable site.

Shortly after the airstrip location was chosen and work had begun on it, I made my weekly trip to the nearest post office located in the town of San Miguel. The people in this town had heard about us and our proposed airstrip. The president of San Miguel wondered if there might not be a suitable place near his town where an airstrip could also be built. We looked at several level places and I described some of the problems involved that would make it difficult to construct an airstrip near his village.

As we were discussing these problems, one of his villagers asked me in a belligerent way why I had chosen to live in San Matías. He evidently had difficulty in understanding why we would pass up his town to live in a town of less prestige and importance. We had based our decision on the fact that Chontal would be spoken more frequently in San Matías, and we wanted to learn the language rather than live in an important town. We did not realize until he asked the question that where we lived had implications for every Chontal village. They considered us to be rich Americans and the airstrip project accentuated that fact. He reacted as strongly as he did because his

A picture of the village of San Matías Petacaltepec taken from the top of the mountain to the east. The Aztec name of the village, Petacaltepec, comes from that mountain.

village of San Miguel, although higher in importance than San Matías, was close enough to be threatened by any increase in the prestige of San Matías. Even Ecatepec, apparently secure enough not to be affected by anything that happened in San Matías, began building an airstrip that has little or no potential use.

Village Relationships

The village of San Matías is spread out for about a half mile along a mountain peak that rises east of the village and shuts off the wind and the view from that direction. Eighty houses, not counting kitchen structures, are either on the ridge itself or its southern slope. The houses on the ridge out-number those on the slope three to one because of the drainage problem from heavy rains. The slope locations do offer the advantage of protection from the northern winds that are strong and cold in the winter months.

The village is divided into two barrios of unequal size with the munici-pal buildings in the middle. The smaller western barrio is only one-fifth the size of the larger eastern one. Each barrio has its own source of water. The water supply for the western barrio is located on the northern slope of the ridge near the eastern limits of the village on the trail to Tequisistlán. The eastern barrio's water supply is on the southern slope near the eastern limits of the village on the trail to Zapotitlán. Both water sources consist of brick and mortar reservoirs about 6 feet in diameter and 3 feet high that collect water from mountain springs or seepage. The water supply for the eastern and larger barrio is more dependable than the other and is used by some of the people from the western barrio when their own water supply is inadequate. If both water sources were to fail, San Matías would probably cease to exist as a village. There is no other nearby source of water on the southern slope and the next water source on the northern slope is quite distant.

The water source on the southern slope is more apt to be contaminated than the other since it is located just below the trail and in the path of waste drainage from the houses above it on the ridge. Both reservoirs have separate, lower reservoirs for livestock to drink from, but they prefer the main reservoirs and their owners allow them to drink from the same reservoir that the people use.

The municipal buildings are located near the western end of the village at the widest part of the ridge. The most imposing structure is the church that has been in the process of being built for over twenty years. Its walls are more than a foot and a half thick, made of stones and mortar. The roof is con-structed of rows of brick and mortar arches. All of the building material used in the church as well as the labor came from San Matías. This is quite an accomplishment because every man in the village is by occupation a farmer first and only a brick or stone mason on a part-time basis. The man who constructed the arched roof was in his sixties and a truly remarkable man. He was self-taught, and no one in the village or in any other mountain village could have duplicated what he has done. The patience and skill involved in such a task is impressive.

Three massive bronze bells hang in the bell tower of the church. Each bell is so heavy that it took a dozen men to lift it into position. One of these bells dates back to the eighteenth century and it staggers the mind to think of all the time and effort it must have taken to move these bells from where they were made to this village—all before the time of trucks and without the use of paved roads.

The school room and teacher's quarters take up most of the northern part of the municipal area. They are made of adobe walls with tile roofs. They have corridors paved with bricks and the roof is supported by brick arches that rest on brick columns. The teacher's quarters consist of a room to live and sleep in, a separate kitchen, and a separate smaller office. The office used to be the village hall where the officials met to discuss their business, but now they have built another hall on the southern edge of the municipal area.

The school room is the longest room in the entire complex and is filled with wooden desks and benches for the students. In the front of the room there is a glass-enclosed flag case in which the Mexican flag is displayed and a large table for the teacher to use. Like all the other rooms, except for the new municipal hall, the school room is plastered inside and out with a type of white plaster. Even with the plaster, the room is rather dark because of the lack of adequate window lighting. The school is the only village building to have win-

The church of San Matías. One of the massive bronze bells is just visible in the bell tower.

dow openings; one on the north side, quite small because of the cold north wind, and another on the south side, much larger but shaded by the corridor. Both window openings have wooden doors on them to close when school is not in session.

To the east of the school is another municipal building that runs north and south and is divided into two rooms. One room is the jail and the other room is empty. The jail is a room about fifteen by twenty feet that has no windows. The only ventilation and light that enter it come through the door which is made of heavy criss-crossed beams spaced close enough to prevent anyone from crawling through them. The door in turn is locked by a heavy chain that is twisted around a pole planted in the corridor.

The empty room was used as a church while the new church was under construction; the room is about three times the length of the jail. It was lined on two sides with wooden statues of various saints riddled with termite holes. At the north end of the room on a raised platform there were three glass encased statues of saints: the patron saint of the village, Saint Matthias; and, flanked on either side of him, two female virgin saints. These three saints are by far the most impressive ones and are clothed in expensive garments; they have since been moved into the newly-finished church.

On the southern rim of the municipal area is the village hall which is also made of adobe. It is the newest building to be added to the municipal complex and is the most modest of any of the buildings. In the center of the municipal area is a basketball court that runs east and west.

The main village trail runs along the ridge that the village is built on and varies in width from six feet on the eastern limits of the village to eighteen feet at its widest point. Wooden crosses set in brick and mortar bases mark the seven stations of the cross taken from Catholic traditions. Near the eastern end of the village is a small structure built of adobe and roofed with aluminum sheeting that was flown in at the request of the man who built the house. It was intended for his personal saint statue but he lacked experience in working with sheeting and he has had to remove the saint because of water leakage.

The cemetery is located west of the village. A few of the individual graves are marked by small brick and mortar plastered structures. Other graves have simpler brick structures made of a few loose bricks while many are not marked at all except for the mound of dirt that has yet to settle on newer graves.

The land that belongs to the village of San Matías lies mostly to the east and covers an area that may be four miles wide at its widest point and eight miles long. Most of the closer village land is owned by individuals, but there is communal land farther away that can be worked by any adult who has paid his taxes. A large plot of land to the east beyond the river is reserved for the use of the school. It is planted in corn and cared for by communal workers. The proceeds go to the school to be used for buying supplies and other school expenses.

In the past the village owned more land but some was sold to the village of San Lorenzo and they lost other land in disputes with neighboring villages. Boundaries consist of either rivers or lanes cleared of trees and under-growth. The lanes tend to be points of friction between villages since they have been changed a number of times in the past. San Matías has had the most trouble to the west with the village of Santa Lucía. In 1959 the men from San Matías went to clear the lane that had begun to grow up in brush. They were met by approximately a half dozen men from Santa Lucía, two of whom were carrying shotguns. The men from Santa Lucía told the villagers from San Matías to go home and allow the lane to grow up in brush. (Santa Lucía has claimed that the lane cuts off land that once belonged to them.) One of the elder citizens of San Matías told his villagers to surround them and take their guns away. They did just that, but they were totally unprepared for the ambush that Santa Lucía had laid for them. Men from Santa Lucía were hidden behind trees and they opened fire with rifles and shotguns loaded with slugs. Three men from San Matías were killed on the spot as well as several of the men from Santa Lucía who had been surrounded and in the line of fire. The people from San Matías ran down the mountain side with bullets and slugs whistling over their heads. They climbed up to their village and began to count their casualties. Besides the three victims, four other men were wounded but were able to escape. The officials from San Matías went to Ecatepec and sent a telegram to Oaxaca informing the government of what had happened. Later they made several trips to Oaxaca to get the matter settled and invested over 3000 pesos in expenses and lawyers' fees to be finally told that they should stay on their land and Santa Lucía should stay on its land. The government in Oaxaca is extremely reluctant to get involved in these land disputes because village boundaries in the state are a matter of constant controversy. It would require armed intervention to make any change. So, there is a large chunk of land today between San Matías and Santa Lucía that no one can use for fear of reprisal.

The main mountain trails that run through land owned by San Matías are maintained by the village in a two-day repair project each year that involves all the men of the village. The trail to Zapotitlán cuts through the airstrip.

The airstrip is located on a north-south ridge about a mile and a half southeast of the village. It represents the biggest investment of time on the part of the villagers in any community project. The strip is only 30 feet wide and 300 feet long but involved extensive digging of the side of a mountain point and filling of a low spot. The only tools that were used were picks, digging bars, shovels, and hoes—mostly hoes. There were no wheelbarrows to move the dirt but some men made carts with wooden wheels. The project began with a great deal of enthusiasm in 1959 but the sheer monotony and size of the task began to discourage most of the villagers before the work was half finished. The village president had difficulty getting people out to work and finally had to appeal to the state representative in Oaxaca for support to convince the men that they should finish the job. The job was not finished until a year later and only one commercial pilot has ever landed on the strip. But the commercial pilot has not found it lucrative enough to interest him in making flights from Oaxaca. He once was paid to fly the school teacher out to the village but high winds prevented him from landing and the village had to pay him 200 pesos for the flight. The airstrip can only be used under ideal conditions because of its substandard length. There are up-drafts, down-drafts, cross winds, and clouds that prevent landing on the strip for too many days out of each year. The strip has been used mostly by the missionary pilot in Mitla who either made flights out at the break of day when there is relatively no wind or called us for a radio report about weather conditions before making the flight.

The airstrip has been a source of ethical conflict for us because the village did the work on it but we profited from it. I never agreed to pay them for any work that they did on it nor did I promise them anything in the way of benefits other than emergency air service for sick people. Only one patient from the village, a young woman having childbirth complications, has been flown out to Mitla. This may have saved her life. Others have preferred to be treated in the village or else we were not there to call the pilot when they were sick. Actually, the Mexican government has set the restrictions on the use of the missionary plane so that it cannot compete with commercial planes in flying passengers or freight. No commercial planes use the strip now and the people of San Matías must be disillusioned at the lack of return on their invest-

The San Matías airstrip. The airplane touches down at the far end and uses the circle at the near end to turn around for its take off.

ment of labor—disillusioned either because of what others had told them would be the benefits of having an airstrip or from their own imaginations. I did buy some picks, bars, and shovels for them halfway through the project because I could see that they were wearing out the few they owned. I also gave the village 1000 pesos at the completion of the airstrip but no one seems to know what happened to it. Next I offered to finance a project to bring running water to the village from a source higher up on the mountain. The conditions that they were to meet included investing 1500 pesos, transporting the materials from the Pan-American Highway, and supplying the labor to dig the ditch. The project would have cost me around 10,000 pesos but it never materialized, perhaps because the women and children carry most of the water in the village and a closer supply of water was not that important to the men. Since then I have given the village various gifts over the years in an attempt to pay off my "debt."

2

Social System

THE PEOPLE WHO INTERACT in the Highland Chontal (hereafter referred to as Chontal) social system can be distinguished from their Zapotecan neighbors by the shape of their heads: the Chontals are more round-headed. They can be distinguished from lowland people who are taller, bigger-boned, and heavier. Chontal men are lean and average five and a half feet in height. The women are a few inches shorter and, although they are more filled out, none of them are excessively fat. Both sexes vary in skin color from light brown to dark brown and have relatively little body hair. The hair on their heads is coarse and varies in color from dark brown to black. They have brown eyes with a hint of oriental characteristics among a few individuals. Many of the adults have a characteristic mountain walk that consists of taking short steps with the body weight shifted slightly forward and restricted arm swing-ing. They are not a handsome people by our standards but they are remarkably adapted to living in their mountain terrain and have developed a workable social system that is worth studying. That system will be described in this chapter in terms of polity, family, and economy.

Polity

ELECTION

Every adult male in his lifetime takes part in a civil–religious political system. The election of village officials takes place each year on the third of November preceding a ritualistic cleaning of the trail just west of the village. When the men reach the halfway point to the village the president stops them and tells them what they already know: it is time to elect the officials for the next year. Cigarettes are passed out to all the men who smoke them before continuing their cleaning job. When they reach the edge of the village the

A Chontal family standing in the corridor of their home. The woman is wearing the traditional huipil *(blouse) and* enagua *(skirt).*

president tells them to gather at the village hall for the election. There the men sit on benches that have been arranged in rows. The most important men sit in the front row or on whatever benches are closest to the president who functions as a chairman. These men are in their fifties, for the most part, and have already served their terms of office as president. Seated behind them are men in their forties and thirties who have held most of the offices in the system except that of alcalde and president. Standing behind them are the youths in their twenties and teens who have just begun to serve in the lowest offices of the hierarchy.

The decisions as to who will serve are made by the men in their fifties, the elders, either ahead of the election meeting or by discussion once the meeting has begun. Although the elders make the decisions, they expect everyone to be present and to discuss the pros and cons of each appointment. These discussions involve several groups of people talking to each other at the same time and so no one can hear everything that is being said. After a while one group after another becomes quiet until only one speaker has the floor.

The first appointment is that of alcalde who is second in command only to the president. The alcalde works closely with the president and his duties are mostly judicial ones. Two helpers and a secretary are elected to serve with him during his term of office. In each case a man's name is proposed by the elders who know which individual has served in the next lower office and is eligible for the proposed office. Or, for the office of secretary, they choose those who can read and write. If there is a consensus of opinion in favor of the one nominated and he cannot present a convincing argument against his serving, he is considered to be elected. There is only one nominee considered at a time and he is usually the one elected by consensus of opinion.

Resistance by a nominee to being elected may occur in respect to any office in the political system, but is usually nothing more than token resistance. The office of president, though, is a job that most men are reluctant to take and some men refuse completely. The reason for their reluctance to serve is that this office, like all the other offices, pays no salary. Unlike the other offices, however, the presidency is expensive. It requires giving a fiesta for the entire village and if someone in charge of a village fiesta does not carry it through, the president may have to step in and be the mayordomo. He must feed the school teacher throughout the school year. The teacher usually expects to be fed a diet similar to what he is accustomed to eating: meat, eggs, rice, and bread—all expensive to buy. The president handles large sums of money and is open to the charge of misusing it or being unable to account for all of it at the end of his term of office. He represents the village to outside officials who speak only Spanish so he must be fairly bilingual and able to deal with outsiders. Some men are not wealthy enough to serve and could not pay back the loans they would be forced to take if they served as president. Others do not have enough of a mastery of the Spanish language and culture to function as representatives of the village. These men are nominated even though it is common knowledge that they will not serve. Perhaps it would be an insult not to nominate them.

The man nominated for president has two ways of refusing to serve.

First, he can let it be known in advance that he will not accept the nomination and will refuse to serve if elected. He can stay away from the election meeting or leave the village ahead of time to convince others that he means what he says. Second, he can appeal to a higher authority, the district town of San Carlos, and pay to be relieved of any further village responsibilities. In either case he will probably be excused because the office of president is an honor that most men would accept, however reluctantly, if there were any possibility of their meeting the qualifications.

After the election of the president, his assistant is elected and also his secretary. Then a man is elected who serves as chief of police. He is in charge of about a half dozen policemen who are chosen from the youngest adults in the community. They begin their service in this lowest office in the hierarchy and they function basically as messenger boys for the president and alcalde. There are another half dozen offices to be filled that fall somewhere in-between the office of police chief and policeman in importance. Finally someone is elected to serve as "Mayordomo of Wax." His task is to oversee the making of candles that takes place once a year at his home at which time he feeds the adult males of the community. Then, too, when there is a school teacher assigned to the village, someone is elected to serve as his helper in school affairs.

DUTIES

The duties of the major officers just mentioned center around the school teacher, community work, the fiesta system, and the legal system. The president is mainly responsible for providing for the needs of the school teacher which range from feeding him to accompanying him on his trips for vacation or to meetings of other school teachers. The school teachers who lived in the village demanded much of the president's time. As a powerful outsider living in the village he could and often did exert more influence than even the president.

I had trouble getting along with the school teachers who were assigned to San Matías for a number of reasons. Each one expected me to give him preferential treatment over the Indians, which I failed to do because of the egalitarian emphasis of the culture from which I had come and also because of the purpose I had in mind—to identify with the Indians. This involved learning their language and it seemed like the hours spent with the school teacher discussing world problems in Spanish did not contribute toward that goal. Each one seemed to resent the fact that I could speak with the Indians in their language—something none of them ever seriously attempted to do. We each resented the other's presence in a situation where one of us would otherwise have been the only outsider. I thought that some of the teachers took advantage of the Indians simply because they were from the dominant outside society. The teachers probably resented the fact that we were foreigners living in Mexico, and rich ones at that, who had airplane and radio service that was not available to them. One teacher went so far as to have published in a Oaxaca newspaper that, although we claimed to be doing language work in San Matías, in reality we were flying out radioactive material to Mitla for commercial purposes. The article caused us some concern but fortunately no one in the government took it seriously.

Each president usually has some project that the community works on during his term of office. This project is decided upon by the elders with the consent of the other males, but it is particularly the project of the man elected president. Those projects since we arrived in the village have involved building an airstrip (two years), the construction of municipal buildings, and building the church. A strong leader as president can mobilize the community and push individuals enough to accomplish a great deal in his own year of office. There is always the pull though of the individual's own personal work that he would like to complete and he resents spending a month or so each year on a community project. A weak leader as president either cannot motivate the community to start on a project or cannot force the individuals to do their part once the project has begun. In both cases he is blamed by the community as being a "do-nothing" president. One man was such a weak president that even one of his relatives talked about having him removed before his term of office was over. Nothing was done though because the elders make the major decisions anyway and they function much the same whether a strong or weak leader is president. Then, too, removing a man from office would cause hard feelings with him and his relatives—something to be avoided if at all possible in a small community. This action would also involve another trip to San Carlos to notify them of the change and the admission that they had elected the wrong man. For these reasons and perhaps others, as far as I know no one has ever been removed from the office of president.

The major office holders are also responsible for the functioning of the fiesta system. There are thirteen fiestas celebrated each year in San Matías: at least one each month except for July and August; three in January and two in June. Each fiesta requires at least one mayordomo with the more significant ones involving two. The biggest fiesta of all is on the twenty-fourth of February for the patron saint of the village. The following is an account of a man who served as mayordomo for that fiesta:

> They gave me the money to be the mayordomo of the fiesta for the twenty-fourth of February. I took it.
> The elders said, 'Take this money. You will be in charge of this fiesta for next year.'
> I said, 'I will do it but find someone else to serve with me first. I don't have any objections to being the mayordomo.'
> Then the elders said, 'We have found one, now let's look for another one.' They found the other one. They said, 'This young man will take the money, now we have the two that we need.'
> My partner said, 'Pick up the money.' We picked it up and counted it. There were 500 pesos there. We tied it up in a handkerchief and took it to my house. When we arrived home, a number of people had followed us and they asked for loans.
> We said, 'If we loan you money you will have to pay the interest on it.' We loaned out the money at the rate of 100 or 200 pesos per man and made a list of those who had the loans.

When it was nine days before the fiesta we bought a cow and slaughtered it. We also bought rockets, cigarettes, and mescal. When the church bell rang we set off our rockets near the church where Mass had been said. Then the people took God out of the church and made a procession through town while we set off some more fireworks. The people took God back into the church and we brought them to our house where we gave them bread and coffee to drink. Then we gave them cigarettes to smoke and mescal to drink while the band played.

On the night before the fiesta we had Mass again and we set off some more fireworks. The band played all night and we fed the people meat broth. The next day we had Mass at the church and then we fed the people again at our house.

Then I said, 'We have finished our jobs as mayordomos. We have the money here that we loaned out with the interest on it.' We put the money on the table and the elders counted it.

Then the elders said, 'Let's look for mayordomos for next year's fiesta.'

In this account there is no mention made of the difficulty in finding someone willing to serve as mayordomo. Usually the proposed mayordomo offers a number of objections to serving since a major fiesta can cost up to 1500 pesos. He cannot save this money by working for someone in the village because no one hires labor for an extended period. Then, too, he would only earn 4 pesos a day which would do little more than pay for the corn that his family needs each day for their tortillas. The only way some men can pay these expenses is to take their family and go work on coffee plantations that are several days' distance from the village. The working conditions there are miserable. Because of having to work in cold rain, what a man makes in wages he often has to pay out in medical treatments for himself and his family. The older men offer the most resistance to serving as mayordomos because they know by experience how much it costs, and some of them have to be insulted before they will serve. Some of them know that they could appeal to the larger Mexican society if they were punished for not participating in what is obviously a religious observance. The younger men are less knowledgeable and yield more readily to the pressure of the elders and the opportunity to gain some social recognition.

The money that is available for loans that is part of the fiesta system continues to grow each year because of the extremely high interest rates. A fiesta loan carries a monthly interest rate of 5 percent or an annual interest rate of 60 percent. Men are still anxious to get these loans, though, because any other loan has an interest rate three to five times as high. A loan to a close friend or relative would have the next lowest interest rate of 15 percent per month or 180 percent per year. Otherwise a man would have to pay back 25 percent interest per month or 300 percent interest per year. All individual loans are backed with collateral so that they must be paid or the creditor seizes the security. Borrowers of fiesta loans are given more leniency when they cannot repay principal plus interest on the due date. Sometimes he is allowed to pay back the interest only and the loan continues for another year. At other times he is made mayordomo for the next year as punishment for failing to honor his loan. If the man is considered to be a poor risk the loan is written off as a lost cause and he will have difficulty borrowing any more fiesta money.

When the fiesta money reaches 1000 or 2000 pesos the bulk of it is used to buy something for the church, such as musical instruments, or something for the school. The remainder stays in the fiesta system.

The indebtedness in a village the size of San Matías is widespread. Out of 120 male adults only about fifteen do not owe money. Of those who owe money some are so hopelessly in debt that they fall further behind each year.

One individual has succeeded in making a small fortune by being the mayordomo for the fiesta of Saint Peter each year. It is not a village-wide fiesta and he keeps his expenses down by feeding the men beans instead of the more expensive meat broth. The invited guests give a small offering to Saint Peter which this man loans out to others at interest. Over the years he has built up a fund of several thousand pesos which he is supposed to use for religious purposes. He did use some of it to put an aluminum roof over a small shelter for Saint Peter but the roof, as mentioned earlier, leaked too much. He has put an aluminum roof over his house which now shelters Saint Peter—the only house besides ours in the village with such a roof.

The entertainment at a fiesta centers on the music played by the village band. The band members are young men in their thirties or younger who are exempted from all other village responsibilities. They have been taught how to play by a band instructor from a neighboring town, and although they are not paid wages as such, they are fed and supplied with cigarettes and mescal at each fiesta celebration. Their instruments belong to the village and repairs or replacements are handled by the village officials. The band members put in especially long and uncomfortable hours during a fiesta when dancing can continue into the cold early hours of the next day. There is discontent among some of the band members either about the condition of their instruments or the long hours involved. Several of them have left the band during the last ten years and none of them have as yet been replaced. One moved to Salina Cruz for the express purpose of being relieved of his band duties and two have left the band for religious reasons but still live in the village.

LEGAL SYSTEM

The major village officials also play the principal judiciary roles in the community. This may involve trying to settle a dispute between the outside government and the village. These affairs are the most difficult for the authorities to handle because they are carried on in written Spanish using a vocabulary and syntax that are poorly understood. The arrival of any letter in the village addressed to the authorities is a matter of uneasy concern, the more so if it is not readily understandable.

Legal matters initiated by outsiders are also troublesome to the village authorities because they involve interacting with Mexicans—a distinct disadvantage for the Indian. For example, two men arrived in San Matías in 1961 claiming to be tax collectors. They told the president that they had come to collect the back taxes that San Matías had failed to pay over the years. They said that they were going to measure each house and the owner would have to pay 3 pesos per meter of length. The only documents that they had with them consisted of a 1949 tax booklet and several letters addressed to the authorities in nearby villages informing them of the purpose of the visit. The village authorities were in a quandry because they knew that their people would resist paying any more taxes and yet these men were insistent that they had been sent to levy these taxes and collect them.

Whenever the village authorities do not want to decide an issue on their own, they call for a town meeting so that everyone will be involved in the decision-making process. I attended the meeting and, in spite of my intentions to stay out of the discussion, I could not sit still and witness the unscrupulous tactics of the two men without saying something. One of the men was the speaker for the two and when he saw that the village was not going to give them permission to levy the tax, he drew up a document that indicted the entire village for tax evasion and rebellion against the government. He forced the village authorities to sign it and he warned them that they would suffer for the way that they had treated him. In spite of his lack of credentials he gave an impressive performance that had the village wondering whether they were doing the right thing in refusing to pay. This uncertainty was not settled until the authorities made a trip to Oaxaca to ask the government officials there about the proposed tax. The other villages that he had "official" letters for had paid him what he had asked. I found out later that he and his partner were wanted by the government for successfully impersonating tax officials and collecting funds from one village after another for their own personal use. They were able to do this because of the reluctance of Mexican Indians to question authorities and legal matters imposed upon them from the larger Mexican society.

Legal matters that involve disputes between villagers are handled by the village authorities themselves without calling for a town meeting. Most of the cases involve fighting between two men who have been drinking and are settled by assessing a fine against the offender and putting him in jail for a night. If it is not possible to determine who is at fault, they both are punished. The amount of the fine varies from 2 to 25 pesos depending on the judgment of the officials and other factors.

The next most frequent offense, after fighting, is disobedience to the village authorities or failure to perform village duties satisfactorily. In one extreme case the alcalde was jailed by the president for a night because he was drinking to excess and not functioning properly in his job. In 1959 a young man was put in jail for not serving acceptably in his village work. He ran away after being jailed but was caught and brought back to be whipped with sticks and then served out his term without any further incidents.

The next most frequent offense is stealing. There is comparatively little stealing of such items as livestock, clothing, or basic foods. Few houses in the village are locked with anything more than a rope tied from the door to a pole. This visible signal of the owner's absence is respected and almost no one would ever attempt to enter such a house. Even when the door is open, the caller waits until he gets a response from his greeting and the invitation to enter before he steps through the door.

Less basic items are stolen frequently, especially if they are located away from the village where detection is not likely. Once I went with a man to pick mangos from some trees he had on a piece of property near the river. When we got there we saw that someone had completely stripped the trees of fruit. He asked a boy who lived on a ranch nearby if he knew who had picked the mangos. The boy either did not know or would not tell and we returned to the village without any fruit.

The most serious punishment is that of carrying heavy rocks for three to five days. In addition, there is a fine and imprisonment in the jail at night for each of the days that he carries rocks. This punishment can be made even more severe by not allowing the prisoner to eat or drink anything for part of this time.

Social relations enter into every legal decision that is made and the desired result is to reach a verdict that is acceptable to all who are involved. If not, the matter will have to be dealt with again because the community is too small for people to be at odds with each other. And so, even if San Carlos were to pass judgment on a matter that favored one of the two individuals involved, the decision would still be unsatisfactory if both individuals were left unreconciled. Then also, as in our society, the poorer and less powerful members of the community are punished more often and more severely for their offenses than are the more influential individuals.

The punishment that is decided upon is meant to have a double effect. The individual involved is punished so that he will not commit the act again. He is also punished so that the other members of the community will be deterred from the same offense. Penalties over the years vary in severity with individual presidents but there does seem to be a trend toward lighter sentences. The most severe sentence that I have a record of occurred in 1945 and was passed on three men who originally came from another town. They lived in San Matías for three years but would not contribute their share of community labor and were troublemakers. They were fined 100 pesos and expelled from the village. The man who was president that year was a strong leader and gave out severe sentences to offenders. He felt that the lighter sentences being given today were one reason why people had less respect for authority. There is always the possibility, though, that the man being punished will hold a grudge against the president and try to get revenge once his term of office is over. The former president tries to explain then that he was acting as president and not as a private citizen when he passed judgment. This type of reasoning has more chance of being accepted if the community believes that the sentence was a just one.

The policemen are not armed with any weapon except a type of billy-club and I have never seen it used on anyone. They serve only one year (as do all the officials) and are extremely reluctant to use force on an offender. Once when they were sent to arrest a young man, he avoided arrest by refusing to go peacefully with them. He had a machete in his hand and in the scuffle that followed the police chief was slightly cut on his hand. The young man broke loose and ran to his ranch where he stayed and avoided arrest. Once a man escapes, no serious attempt is made to pursue him. That kind of pursuit would involve a number of policemen for a longer period of time than they are willing to spend in their service to the village. Each policeman is first a farmer and is called from his work each time that the officials have a task for him to perform; understandably he wants to get the task over as soon as possible and get back to his farming.

In the instance of the young man just described, an older man in the community took it upon himself to go and reason with him. He explained to the young man that he would only cause trouble for himself if he continued to refuse to obey the authorities. This type of reasoning prevailed and the young man was soon functioning again in the social system.

Their legal system works effectively because it is reinforced by the entire social system. Children are taught the values of their parents and are impressed with the importance of conforming to the expectations of others. If they do not conform, they are ridiculed by their peers and it is believed that the embarrassment suffered by the individual being laughed at can cause him to become sick. If he persists in deviating from approved conduct, he is considered to be a troublemaker and is open to accusations of practicing witchcraft.

The value system will be discussed more in detail later in this book but one theme that is constantly stressed is that a good man does not cause trouble. The fights that occur almost invariably follow excessive drinking during a fiesta when the controls that hold in check the tensions of living in any community are relaxed.

Many legal cases are never brought before the authorities because they are handled by the individuals themselves who are involved. One such case involved the burro of our former landlord in the village. His wife had taken the burro out to feed and had tied him so that he would not get into someone's fields. She returned to the village and a few hours later a child came running to tell her that her burro was dead. We all went out to the place where he had been tied and it was obvious that he had been in a fight with another burro. The only burro running loose that was capable of killing this burro belonged to another man in the village. The two parties got together and agreed upon a fair price for indemnification which settled the case without referring it to the village authorities.

Sometimes an individual who feels that he has been wronged and cannot get satisfaction in any other way will resort to retaliation. This happened to our former landlord who was trying to help us buy a house near his. The house had been owned by a man who became sick and died soon after he had built it. He left no close relatives except a commonlaw wife and a son by an earlier marriage. She was paid what she thought was a fair price for her interest in the house and the guardian of the boy was paid an equal amount but the boy, who was about twelve years of age, was not agreeable to the sale of the house. One morning our former landlord saw that one of the two bulls that he kept tied at night near his house was crippled. He called a friend of his and they decided to kill the bull before it died of sickness so that the meat would still be edible. In the process of skinning the animal they discovered that he was not sick but had been beaten so severely that he was crippled. No one had seen the beating take place but it was common knowledge that it had been done by an uncle of the boy who did not want the house sold. The issue was not pushed any further and the house was not sold to anyone until after the boy left the village.

Family

The kinship system of these people is quite different from our own kinship system and a comparison of the two will be made to help explain the Chontal system. Kinship systems can be broken down into the basic semantic elements that characterize the system and compose each kinship term. The consanguineal or blood relative terms of the U.S. system according to Wallace and Atkins (1960) consist of these components: sex of relative (a), generation (b), and lineality (c). Sex of relative has two subdivisions: male (a_1), or female (a_2). Generation has five or more subdivisions: grandparent (b_1), parent (b_2), ego (b_3), child (b_4), and grandchild (b_5). Lineality has three subdivisions: lineal (c_1), colineal (c_2) and ablineal (c_3). Lineal relatives are ancestors or descendants of ego. Colineal relatives are: (1) nonlineals all of whose ancestors are also ancestors of ego (i.e., uncle, aunt, brother, sister), or (2) nonlineals of whom all the ancestors of ego are also their ancestors (i.e., niece, nephew). Ablineal relatives (i.e., cousins) are neither lineal nor colineal relatives. They are not colineal relatives because they do not meet either of the two conditions listed above: (1) their ancestors (i.e., uncle, aunt) are not ancestors of ego; (2) not all the ancestors of ego (i.e., ego's mother and father) are their ancestors.

The consanguineal terms of the U.S. kinship system can then be charted as follows:

	c_1			c_2		c_3	
	a_1	a_2		a_1	a_2	a_1	a_2
b_1	grandfather	grandmother					
b_2	father	mother		uncle	aunt		
b_3			ego	brother	sister		cousin
b_4	son	daughter		nephew	niece		
b_5	grandson	granddaughter					

The term *grandfather*, for example, consists of these components: $a_1 b_1 c_1$; it is the only kinship term having those components. The term *cousin* has these components: $a\ b\ c_3$, with no subscript indicated for a or b because this term does not identify the sex or generation of the referent, the only such instance in the system.

The componential elements of the Chontal consanguineal terms are:

sex of relative (a), age of relative (b), and lineality (c). Sex of relative has two subdivisions: the sex of the relative is the same as that of ego (a_1); the sex of the relative is different from that of ego (a_2). Age of relative has two subdivisions: the relative is older than ego (b_1); the relative is younger than ego (b_2). Lineality has two subdivisions: lineal relatives (c_1)(as defined under the U.S. system) and nonlineal relatives (c_2).

The consanguineal terms of the Chontal system can be charted as follows for a male ego:

	c_1		c_2	
	a_1	a_2	a_1	a_2
b_1	kay-ʔáyiʔ	kay-ʔmámaʔ	łáy-wił'	łay-šʔápi
	(father)	(mother)	(uncle)	(aunt)
	ego			
b_2		łáy-ʔwa		łaypíma
		(son, daughter)		(brother, sister)

There are several important differences between these two sets of kinship terms. First, the U.S. system has terms for five generations as compared with two for the Chontal system. The Chontal system, on the other hand, stresses differences in relative age between ego and the referent that can be less than a generation. Whereas the chart for the U.S. terms would not change if ego were either a male or female, the chart for the Chontal terms would have to be changed by substituting łay-nenóta for łáy-wił' if ego were a female. And finally, the U.S. system has three degrees of lineality as contrasted with two in the Chontal system. Because of the generational emphasis of the U.S. chart plus the three degrees of lineality this system could be called an isolating one. The Chontal chart collapses both the generational and the lineality distinctions of the U.S. chart and thus could be called a combining kinship system.

These terminological distinctions have social implications for both societies. The U.S. generational terms are part of an inheritance mechanism that passes wealth on to the descendants of ego. This passage of wealth contributes to social differences in a society that gives prestige status to the rich. The lack of this type of generational differentiation in the Chontal terms is accompanied with a relative lack of concern about inheritance. The Chontal social system is much more egalitarian and the accumulation of wealth which results in social differentiation is not encouraged. Social differentiation calls attention to individuals and this is to be avoided because it can provoke jealousy. Jealousy, in turn, can result in sickness to the individual who is envied. Charges of being in league with the devil are also made against rich individuals by poorer people who are reluctant to admit that they do not work as hard or as intelligently as those who are rich. Then, too, rich people are sometimes killed for their wealth and their possessions are divided up. This happened to a storekeeper from a neighboring village who was on his way down to the valley towns to buy supplies. He was ambushed near San Matías and murdered for his money. No one has been apprehended for the murder. People are understandably reluctant to give any indication that they have money on their person or anywhere else.

The stress on the importance of relative age and sex in the Chontal system is a major part of the basis for status in this ascription-oriented society. The most respected Chontal is an elderly male; the least respected is a girl. A Chontal is respected more for who he is than what he may have accomplished. The importance of old age gives the society an orientation toward the past and a corresponding conservatism toward change. This conservatism is reinforced by the belief that on the fiesta of Todos Santos the deceased are expected to return to their former families to see if things are still being done in the time honored way. The reverse of this is true of the U.S. achievement-oriented society where an individual is honored not so much for who he is in terms of sex and age but for what he has acquired in wealth or accomplished through his occupation. He is given respect through the use of various occupational titles such as Doctor, Professor, or Reverend. Or, he is given preferential treatment as a rich person because of his conspicuous display or consumption of wealth. In the Chontal society, a person who is not a relative is treated with respect by using the terms for uncle (*máy-wiⁱ*) and aunt (*may-šʔápi*) in addressing them. Respected men are called first to eat at a fiesta so that each fiesta reinforces the social distinctions of the society. These men are the ones who sit nearest the president and make the decisions that affect the entire village. They walk ahead of others on a mountain trail and kneel closest to the village gods during the church services.

The three degrees of lineality in the U.S. terms coupled with the generational differentiation gives the system an isolating and individual orientation. The social structure supports this isolation with small nuclear families that are composed ideally only of parents and children with intense emotional ties. The other relatives are sharply differentiated from those of the nuclear family and not only do not live with the family but are not supposed to interfere in such family affairs as disciplining the children. When a young man marries in our society he is expected to form a new household which may or may not be in the same city as that of his parents. Not only would he be accused of lack of ambition if he did not move away from home when he married, but his parents would be considered economic failures if they ever moved in with one of their married children. The Chontal terms have only two degrees of lineality; cousins are grouped together with uncles, aunts, brothers, and sisters. This combining characteristic is also supported by the social system that has a group orientation. Instead of the neolocal residence pattern of the newly married in the U.S. society, a young man has his wife move in with his parents in a patrilocal residence pattern. There is no separation of his family of orientation in which he is raised from his new family of procreation until several years have passed. There often are other relatives living with his parents so that he is raised in an extended family without the intense emotional ties to his parents that are characteristic of the U.S. family. These other relatives help to raise him and, if his mother or father should die, a relative could function as the deceased parent. Even when the young man moves away from his parents' home he often builds a house next to the house of his parents. Seldom does he ever leave the village of his parents, and those who do are never fully accepted in another mountain village. His village is always the village where he was born and raised, no matter how long he might have lived as an adult in another village.

The household composition of San Matías reflects the combining aspect of the Chontal kinship system in that about half of the homes consist of extended families which vary in size from three to eleven people. An example of the preference that these people have for living in extended families is that of our former landlord. He and his wife had built the largest house in town that consisted of two rooms. He insisted soon after we arrived in town that we should live in one of the rooms and they would live in the other. This arrangement was probably the best possible one for us since we had someone to help us over the rough spots in our first attempts at learning the language and culture of these people. Later we felt that we should move into a house of our own, and after we did, this man and his wife were evidently lonesome. He went down to the valley and talked a former San Matías resident into returning with his family and sharing the house where we once lived. They have lived together now for several years and both families seem satisfied with an arrangement that would not even be considered as an option by most Americans.

Relatives provide a type of social security to a Chontal who is taken care of by older relatives when he is growing up and then later provides care for those same relatives when they are too old to be self-sufficient. In addition to his consanguineal relatives and those acquired through marriage, he can extend his circle of relatives through ritual terms introduced through the Catholic church. These terms include Spanish equivalents for co-father, co-mother, godfather, godmother, and godchild. Besides the traditional responsibilities of providing for a child who has lost one or both of his parents or needs help in a predicament, co-parents expect and receive preferential treatment from each other. This may involve nothing more than greeting one another with the appropriate co-parent term in public or it can extend all the way to selling items cheaper and loaning money at a lower rate of interest than would be done to someone else. Ritual terms are used more conspicuously than the kinship terms and one gets the impression that co-parents never miss the opportunity to address each other in public and godchildren also make a point of addressing their godparents. A Chontal may have up to a half dozen co-parents scattered throughout the various mountain villages and this provides him with a place to stay when he attends a fiesta in one of those villages. Some co-parent relationships are more important than others depending on the compatibility of the individuals involved. They continue to interact long after all parental responsibilities have ended.

COURTSHIP AND MARRIAGE

Courtship and marriage are interfamily concerns among the Chontals. The son initiates the action by asking his father to talk to the family of the girl he wants to marry. He will be in his late teens and the girl he wants to marry will probably be in her early teens or even younger. Brides this young are desired because they have not yet begun to menstruate. There is the belief that a girl has had sexual intercourse with someone if she starts to menstruate. Because of this belief, menstruating unmarried girls keep their condition secret, even from their own parents.

A young man may have serious problems in finding a suitable mate within his village for a variety of reasons. Marrying someone from another village is a possibility but it is discouraged. First, there are localized lineage aspects in the organization of each village and a distinction is made between "legitimate" town members (those born in the village) and "outsiders" who never seem to be completely accepted. Then, too, residence is ideally patrilocal and mothers hesitate to allow their daughters to move away from the village.

The magnitude of the problem of finding an eligible mate can be seen by taking a specific boy and tracing the status of each marriageable girl in the village. It was found that there were thirty-two girls of marriageable age in San Matías. The consanguineal kinship system reduced this number to twenty-four, since the term łay-píma (my brother/sister) is applied to all siblings and cousins on both the paternal and maternal sides. This results in a situation where the boy cannot consider anyone as a prospective mate who is closer than a fourth cousin.

The affinal system reinforces this extension of the term łay-píma to the marriage partner of such a relative even though the relative may be a distant cousin of the boy.

The ritual terms further reduce the number of marriage prospects by ruling out families that are linked ritually. Thus if the boy's father is a co-parent with the father of the girl in question, she is not an eligible mate. This practice reduces the boy's prospects to eighteen.

When families address each other with the appropriate consanguineal term, distant relationships are kept alive that might otherwise be forgotten. The boy in question then can never marry into the other family, no matter how distant a cousin the girl may be. This custom reduces the number of the boy's potential mates to ten. Of these ten girls, all but three are either too old (too far past puberty) or too young to be ideal wives. Thus the four criteria mentioned above, plus an ideal marriage age, drastically reduce the boy's choices of a marriage partner. The kinship system that extends its ties to include so many distant relatives has the accompanying disadvantage of making it more difficult for a young man to marry. And of course, nothing has been said as yet concerning the preferences of the girls and their families. It is quite conceivable that the boy in focus will not appear at the head of any of their lists and will have to select a spouse who is less than ideal according to one of the criteria (for example, preferred age) where there is flexibility.

Once a potential mate has been identified, the father of the boy calls at the house of the girl on a Saturday evening. After visiting with the parents of the girl for an hour or so, he introduces the subject. He is given a stereotyped answer to return in a week while they ask the girl what her wishes are. The man returns the next Saturday and asks what has been decided. He is told that she still hasn't made up her mind and he should come back again the next Saturday. When he returns he may be told that they are willing to have their daughter marry his son. But, they want to make sure that the boy really loves their daughter so they would like to have him bring his son with him on the next Saturday. The father and son return the following Saturday and the father of the boy asks if they are agreeable to the marriage. The parents of the girl say that they are and then they accept gifts of cigarettes, bread, mescal, and cakes of pressed chocolate to seal the agreement. Early the next Saturday the groom's parents begin to prepare a wedding feast of meat broth, tortillas, atole, bread, and coffee. In the evening they, their son, and the village authorities go to the house of the girl. The boy's mother has taken with her a complete change of clothing for the bride. The girl undresses down to her underclothing in the presence of both sets of parents and the wedding guests, which include the godparents of the girl and relatives. The boy's mother then dresses the girl with the clothes she has brought. Up to this time the girl has worn dresses but now she may be dressed in the costume worn by the women. Their clothing consists of a blouse with three-quarter length sleeves worn over a *huipil*. The *huipil* has short sleeves and is elaborately embroidered in a geometric design on front and back. They wear a full skirt called a *nagua de olan* that reaches to within a few inches of the ground. The bottom of the skirt has a white ruffle that is removable for washing. The mother of the boy may bring a dress instead of the traditional costume which the girl will wear until she becomes pregnant. When she "begins to show" she will then change to the costume. The boy's mother also brings a new pair of *huaraches* or sandals for the girl as well as a new necklace and earrings. She combs the girl's hair and braids it with the new hair ribbons that she has brought and gives her a long black scarf made of silk and fringed with tassels. While the bride is being dressed in one corner of the room, the wedding guests have been offered mescal and cigarettes by the boy's father. Once the bride is dressed, the candles brought by the godparents are lit and given to the boy and girl who lead the procession to the boy's house. The guests are fed the food that has been prepared and then the bride and groom kneel before the household saints while the village authorities tell the bride what is expected of her now that she is married:

Be sure and do what they tell you to do here and work hard. Get up early and grind corn and cook atole. Serve the food to your husband and your new mother and father. Work hard with what you have. You have heard that we have told you to get up early because your man has his work. He has to get up early to get it done. When he gets home in the evening, you should have his tortillas and food cooked for him. Feed him his supper and give him his tortillas. Obey what they tell you to do here. That is what we are telling you.

When the authorities have finished their advice to the bride, they leave with the other wedding guests.

Later, when the Catholic priest who lives in the lowland village of Huamelula visits San Matías, the couple may decide to have a church service as

One of the more expensive homes in San Matías. The separate structure to the left is used for a kitchen.

well. This is as far as most couples go but they are still not married in a civil sense until they go to San Carlos and are married by an official there.

The newly married couple will sleep on a bed made of freshly cut bamboo poles that are strung together with cord and supported by two benches placed at each end of the poles. The boy has cut the poles earlier in the day and carried them back to his home where he laced them together with cord. If the boy believes strongly in the traditions of his elders, he may wait from three to nine days before he has intercourse with his bride. During that time he will fast until noon and not smoke or drink while he hires someone to make the appropriate offerings to the various gods of the earth. The newlyweds often sleep in the same room with the rest of the family but may also sleep separately in the kitchen.

HOUSES

Chontal houses consist of two rooms or two completely separate structures. The main house is made of whatever materials the owner can afford. The poorest people have houses whose walls consist of bamboo poles that are lashed or braided to three horizontal poles. Mud daubing may then be applied inside and out to make a solid wall. The roof of this type of house is of grass tied in bunches with vines to horizontal bamboo poles that in turn are tied to wooden poles. These wooden poles meet at the top and are tied there with vines to a ridge pole. They rest on horizontal poles which are supported by the four cornerposts of the house. This type of house has a door made of bamboo poles strung together with cord and a dirt floor. The grass roof allows smoke to escape and the family often does their cooking in this room and not

Part of the interior of a Chontal home. Note the ears of corn stacked up behind the sewing machine and the squash lying underneath the bench.

in a separate kitchen. The grass roof has certain advantages over any other type of roof. If it is in good repair, it does not leak during a long rainy spell as tile often does. And, it muffles the sound of a hard rain in contrast to a metal roof. The only disadvantage to having a grass roof is the threat of fire, not so much from the fire used for cooking, but from the rockets that are shot off during fiestas and that sometimes land on a grass roof before they are burned out.

The next type of house has adobe walls made of sunbaked adobe with mud used for mortar. This house has a grass roof that rests on the top of the adobe walls with a door made of wood that turns on hinges and can be locked with a key.

The last type of house has adobe walls, a tile roof, a wooden door, a floor made of bricks or cement, and a corridor. The corridor extends the length of the house and is supported by brick columns. This type of house may contain two rooms neither of which is used for a kitchen. Instead, one room might be used as a store or as sleeping quarters for part of the extended family. The other room might be used as sleeping quarters for the rest of the family or as a storeroom for their corn, beans, and other supplies. The furniture in the main room consists of benches placed along the walls and a bed supported by benches. There may also be shaped blocks of wood to sit on and, if there are any chairs, they tend to be quite low since most people place their dishes on the floor for their meals. Every main room has a saint table on which the household saint is placed between candles and flowers. There is usually a wooden chest that contains documents or valuables and can be locked. The wealthier homes have a sewing machine and a portable radio or phonograph with a gasoline lamp to use for special occasions. To keep clothing from getting mildewed it is hung over one or two ropes that are strung from one wall to another of the house.

Kitchens do not show the variability found in the main house structures and are almost all made of bamboo walls. Most of the kitchens have grass roofs but some of them have tile roofs supported by bamboo so that the smoke can escape. Kitchens tend to be smaller than the main room of the house, which varies in size from 11 by 19 feet to 10 by 12 feet. The kitchen contains a fireplace that is always in one corner of the room and may either be on the floor or on a raised adobe platform. The fireplace consists of rocks arranged in a semicircle and on which is placed a large clay griddle that is used for baking tortillas. Corn is boiled in a bucket suspended with a wire tied to the handle. The wire is fastened on the other end to a beam over the fireplace.

Near the fireplace is a corn grinder that costs about 40 pesos and is clamped on a post. The corn is first boiled in lime water, then washed several times in a sieve made out of a half gourd with holes punched in. After draining the corn, it is put through the corn grinder but is still not of the proper consistency to be made into a tortilla. The grinding process is finished on a *metate*, a large flat stone that has been partially hollowed out. Another smaller stone called a *mano de metate* is held in the hands of the woman and stroked back and forth, grinding the corn dough even finer. The woman then shapes the corn dough in her hands into a large pancake or tortilla, about 12 to 14 inches in diameter. The tortilla is then baked on the large clay griddle.

These are the main items in the kitchen but there are also a variety of pots and pans used in cooking plus various buckets of different sizes. Gourds used as water containers, bowls, or strainers are also present along with a fire blower made out of a piece of bamboo. The bamboo is hollowed out except for the plug on the end which has a small hole drilled through it and is directed at the spot where the person wants to blow.

The kitchen is either lit at night by the fire in the fireplace or by pitch pine sticks, the cheapest lighting available. Next cheapest is a kerosene lamp made out of a tin can with a small opening through which a rope-like wick is inserted. A kerosene lantern gives off more light than the tin can lamp but costs about 25 pesos. The most powerful and expensive lighting is a pressure gasoline or kerosene lantern that costs about 200 pesos.

BIRTH

Childbirth is the most prevalent cause of death among women so there is a great deal of anxiety associated with it. The pregnant woman often does not know of her condition until she feels the baby move. Once it is known that she is pregnant there are a number of taboos that she should not break. She is not to walk in the river or a spirit-being will eat the child. She is considered to have dangerous power that is not under her control so that her mere presence can ruin the process of making bricks, sugar, or lime.

She is supposed to follow a bland diet that includes no meat and in the final months of pregnancy she is told to eat less so that her baby will not be too fat to be born. Unfortunately some women eat so little that their children are born sickly and soon die.

Just before the woman is ready to give birth, her husband will either perform the appropriate ritual for childbirth or pay someone else to do it so that there will be no complications in birth. The birth takes place in the house and precautions are taken to make sure that the expectant mother is kept warm. The door of the house is shut to keep out the wind and cold air and hot coals are placed under the bamboo bed that the woman is lying on. She is bundled in several blankets with a scarf about her head. This preoccupation with heat is due to their fear of the woman getting chilled, one of the first symptoms of massive childbirth infection. They do not understand the concept of infection, but they do recognize its symptoms and try to guard against it. If the woman has a prolonged delivery, she sweats so much under these conditions that she loses her strength.

Assisting her will be her husband, mother, and possibly a midwife. As soon as the childbirth pains are severe, the woman kneels on the floor with her legs spread apart on a straw mat. Her husband is seated on a chair or bench and she grasps him around his waist while he helps to support her with his knees against her sides. The midwife sits behind the woman and pushes on the woman's back and catches the baby when he falls. This position for the woman is the most natural one that she can assume both for the delivery of the baby and the expulsion of the placenta, but is very tiring in prolonged labor.

As soon as the baby is born the mother continues in the same position until the placenta is expelled. Then a long sash is quickly tied around her waist and she is put to bed, wrapped in blankets. During this time the baby is unattended, shivering on the straw mat in his afterbirth. Once the mother has been attended to, he is picked up and his cord is tied about eight inches from his stomach with a piece of thread or string. Then the cord is cut with a piece of sharp bamboo. Nothing made of metal is used because there is the belief that the use of metal will make the baby have a mean disposition. Actually, the use of bamboo is preferable to metal but for a different reason: there is less danger of infection with bamboo than unsterilized metal. Next the baby is washed in cold water and a piece of cloth is wrapped tightly around the umbilical cord and his stomach. He is then wrapped in a shawl and put to bed with his mother who will spend from one to four weeks in bed. She resumes her duties so slowly because she is afraid that she might bleed to death otherwise. The mother will eat only foods that are considered hot in the Chontal classification of foods. These foods will be heated before they are served to her so that nothing cold enters her body.

If the birth process is prolonged at all, both mother and child will probably die. The mother will die from childbirth infection caused by internal bruising, lowered resistance, and unsanitary conditions. The baby will die from being born in a weakened condition or strangled by his own cord. As soon as any trouble is experienced in the birth process, a number of remedies are used. The woman may be given various preparations to drink made of hot pepper, soot scraped from above the fireplace, ground-up deer bones, or cactus juice. The midwife will attempt to move the child into a different position by pushing gently with her hands against the mother's womb. If that fails, several men will pick the woman up by her feet and jerk her in a final attempt to change the position of the child in her womb. Pressure may be applied to her womb to force the birth of the child and, if all else fails, a midwife will pull the child out of the womb with her own hands. The child is probably dead now but an effort is made to save the mother's life. She, however, is usually suffering from internal damages by this time and, without the use of antibiotics, will die.

Some women are so concerned about having children that they drink various herbs that are supposed to prevent conception. One woman drank powdered mule's foot as a contraceptive since mules do not have offspring. Her remedy was just as ineffective as the other contraceptives that are used and she soon became pregnant.

Other women are concerned about their failure to have children, and with good reason, since this is cause enough for a man to leave his wife. Since almost no one is married in a civil sense, divorce is not a legal matter that goes beyond the village itself. If a man and woman are childless or incompatible in some way, they reach a decision to separate and, unless property is involved, the matter is not brought before the village authorities. Either partner is then free to live with someone else without benefit of another marriage ceremony. The barren woman, though, will have a difficult time finding another husband, for men want children, preferably boys, who will honor and remember them when they are dead. Childless women drink herbs that are supposed to cure their sterility and make pilgrimages to the shrines of saints that are reputed to answer the prayers of sterile women. One woman made a baby rag doll and tied it inside her skirt and wore it there for nine days before Christmas one year, reading a prayer each day. She failed to become pregnant and later her husband took her to a doctor down in the valley. He treated her but she is still barren and their marriage continues to be precarious.

CHILDHOOD

Babies are raised under what would impress us as being permissive child training practices. The baby either sleeps in bed with his mother or in a small mesh hammock near the mother's bed. As soon as he begins to cry an attempt is made to pacify him and if the mother is present, she will begin nursing him. If the mother is out, an older woman relative will let the baby suck on one of her empty breasts until the mother returns. The baby is dressed, male or female, with a wrap-around skirt that is tied around his waist. He is carried in a shawl that is tied around the neck and shoulders of his mother and supports him like a hammock. He can be carried on the back of his mother in this shawl or quickly switched to the front and given a breast when he gets hungry.

No attempt is made to discipline a baby nor is there any reason to stress toilet training since the baby does not wear diapers and there is nothing he can damage through soiling. He will become continent later at his own pace with teasing from his peers if he is unusually slow. His parents speak to him in baby talk and call him indulgently, "papa" or "mama," according to his sex.

His last name will usually be that of his father and his first name will be given to him by his parents, often taking the saint's name of his birthdate. His parents will ask another couple of their choice to be his godparents and when the priest visits the village, the chosen godfather will hold the baby while the priest baptizes him. Until the time of his baptism the baby is a nameless being who is not mourned with the same intensity if he dies as he would be if he had been baptized.

Little boys are given preferential treatment over little girls in a family by allowing the boy to eat with his father while the little girl eats with her mother after the males have been served. Boys are dressed in shirt and pants once they are toilet trained and girls at the same time begin to wear dresses with or without underclothing.

Children start school at about six or seven years of age and stop in their early teens but few have ever gotten beyond the first three grades because of a number of factors. In the past there have been years when no teacher was hired, or one teacher was expected to teach sixty children in a one-room school building. Pressure has to be applied to some families to send their children because they cannot see the need for schooling, especially for the girls in their family. Boys who can read and write can serve as secretaries in the town hall, but girls are not elected to that office and there seems to be no useful function served by teaching them to read. For either sex there is such a scarcity of reading material that they never develop the skills that they are taught in school.

Boys play games that are more competitive than those played by girls and include basketball, shooting marbles, and playing tag. Girls play games that are more directly related to what they will be doing as grownups. They have rag dolls that they sew clothes for out of scraps of material. Their mothers will allow them to practice shaping corn dough in their hands into tortillas which are then baked on the family's clay griddle. Both boys and girls carry water from the well for the family's needs but girls are expected to begin earlier in helping out with adult work. They help to shell corn and grind it for atole gruel or for making tortillas. Girls also are expected to look after younger children and they often carry them around in a shawl on their backs as their mothers do.

ADOLESCENCE

By the time children reach adolescence they have been informally taught the occupational roles that they will perform as adults. They now work alongside their fathers and mothers in the field and the girls are an important help to their mothers in preparing the food that the family eats. Parents guard their daughter's virginity by making sure that she is not alone with a boy at any time. When she is sent on an errand her little brother or sister accompanies her as a deterrent to any illicit affairs. These family safeguards are effective for most of the girls but the school situation is something that falls outside parental supervision. In one instance the teacher had assigned a boy and a girl to sweep out the school each morning. Another girl happened to come to school early one morning and saw the two having intercourse on the schoolroom floor. The two saw her also and the girl involved told her parents that she had been seen having intercourse. Her parents went and talked to the parents of the girl who had witnessed the act and pleaded with them not to tell anyone about it or their daughter might have a difficult time getting married.

The big social event for young people is the fiesta when they can get dressed up and dance together. In their older form of dancing the couple faces each other but without touching one another. Most of the movement is from the waist down with small steps in rather deliberate movements. Their faces are expressionless without the trace of a smile nor do they look directly at each other. In the newer form of dancing they hold each other but never closely and there is still the restraint present that characterizes the older way of dancing. Restrictions are relaxed somewhat during fiestas and sexual encounters are more likely to take place than at other times.

Basketball is the main activity that teenage boys have for recreation and San Matías has four or more teams that have their own uniforms, basketballs, and whistles. During the afternoon of a fiesta, these teams will play other teams from neighboring villages for prizes or just for fun. Teenage girls may be chosen as "queens" for the occasion and will award the prizes to the victorious team members. These games are timed and once in a while a game will end in a tie. The reaction is almost one of relief and nothing is done to break the tie; it is considered a satisfactory way to end a game.

ADULTHOOD

Men are divided into the two broad classes of elders and offspring. Elders are those who are in their late forties and above, most of whom have served as president. The offspring category includes men in their early forties and below who have not served as president. Both elders and offspring are expected to do communal work and pay their village taxes but when a man is in his sixties and no longer wants to function in village affairs he is allowed to "retire." These old men continue to work their fields as long as they have strength left.

At one time in the past these old men were treated with more respect than they are today. A young man when meeting an old man used to step aside, fold his arms, bow slightly, and say, "Hello, father." The old man would reply, "Hello, child," as he continued on his way. It was believed that the younger man would stumble, fall, and die if he passed by without showing this respect to the old man. And it used to be that when an old man passed by, people would comment, "Our father-god passed by." These greetings are no longer used and young people feel somewhat embarrassed even to use the term *máy-wil'* "my uncle" in addressing an older man but instead use the Spanish word *tío* "uncle" or nothing at all.

Old people today are miserable once they can no longer provide for their own needs because they realize they are a burden on their younger relatives. The ones who live unusually long are considered to be dangerous because they have not died and they suffer from accusations of witchcraft.

Women are divided less formally into two classes of young and old. Women beyond childbearing are considered to be old and the extremely old ones wear an identifying denim wrap-around skirt. Old women are respected more than young women but neither are respected as much as men. Women are either not fed at fiestas or food is taken to their houses after all the men have been fed. Women kneel outside the church or in the back of the church and when they are called down to the town hall, they stand outside the office to talk to the authorities who are seated inside. Women are not always given the same legal considerations as men and a married woman may have trouble inheriting her deceased husband's property if he has close male relatives who want to contest the settlement.

DEATH

Babies who have not been baptized are not mourned because it is believed that they do not have souls until they are baptized. Everyone else who dies is mourned by his family and relatives who gather at his house. All dead people are dressed in their best clothes and wrapped in a straw mat (*petate*). If the deceased is a man, a gourd of water and tortillas in a carrying net are placed in the straw mat for his journey into the afterlife. If the deceased is a woman, a gourd of water and tortillas wrapped in a cloth are included as well as a comb, needle and thread, and mending cloth.

The village band and cantors celebrate the Mass at the home of the deceased while the close relatives feed those who have come. Then a procession is formed to accompany the body to the church where incense is blown over the body and it is sprinkled with salt water. The deceased is then taken to his grave in the village cemetery.

The grave is about 5 feet deep and just wide enough to allow the body to be lowered into it. After the body is laid in the grave, a platform made of boards or poles is put into place about a foot above the body. Then the loose dirt is shoveled in and the grave is mounded up with the remaining dirt. If the deceased is a child, his toys are placed on the grave along with kernels of corn and several bowls. The tools used are washed with water and also the hands of those who used them. Then the mourners, along with the band and cantors, return to the village.

The soul of the deceased is believed to wander around the village until nine days later when a Novena is observed. The mourners who arrive at the home of the deceased for the Novena are fed again while the band and cantor celebrate a Mass. Then they form a procession to the grave where incense is burned to carry the soul up to heaven. On the fiesta of Todos Santos, the village authorities with the band, cantors, and other members of the community go to the cemetery. The authorities then invite all the deceased ones to return to the village and eat the bread and tamales that have been set out for them by their relatives. After the deceased ones have eaten the "essence" of this food and have had a chance to look around the village, they are returned to the graveyard in a procession. The living relatives return to their village taking with them the food that had been placed on the graves of their loved ones. This food is then eaten along with any other food that had been offered to the deceased ones.

The graveyard is avoided at night and the dead are feared because if they are not satisfied with the way their relatives are living when they visit the village on Todos Santos, they might decide to take the living with them. The deceased, then, are a factor for conservatism and against change, especially change in ideology or religion.

Economy

The economy of any society sets the limits in which social and cultural elaboration can take place. A description of the society's economy then is basic to an understanding of the society itself. The two most important components of an economy are its technological complexity and division of labor.

TECHNOLOGICAL COMPLEXITY

There are only two sources of energy that are used in the Chontal system: animals and humans. Animals carry loads of firewood, corn, maguey stumps from which mescal is made, mescal, grass, bricks, and tiles. These load-bearing animals are burros, horses, and mules. A burro costs about 300 pesos when grown and can carry about 100 pounds of cargo over mountain trails. Horses cost from 400 to 500 pesos and can carry approximately 150 pounds. A mule costs up to 1000 pesos and carries no more than 200 pounds in these mountains. All of these animals are smaller than animals raised down in the valley—the long term result of poor nutrition. Besides these load-bearing animals, a few people own oxen that are used to turn the gears of a sugar press. Full-grown oxen sell for 1000 pesos.

These animals require what the Chontals consider to be quite a bit of care. The animals have to be taken out to pasture each day by those living in the village and brought back again each night. They have to be taken far enough away from cornfields and sugar cane patches so that they do not wander into them. The fines levied against the owners of animals that cause damage to these crops are heavy, excessive in my opinion, and discourage the raising of stock.

The biggest discouragement in raising and owning these animals is a paralytic type of rabies that occurs in epidemic cycles. It is always fatal and is spread by the blood sucking vampire bat. The afflicted animal gets stiff in his hind quarters, begins to stagger, goes down, and never gets up again. The whole process lasts less than a week and there is nothing that can be done for the infected animal to halt the disease. He can be vaccinated against it but this must be done each year at a cost of 10 to 15 pesos and I know of no one who is willing to do this until the next epidemic strikes, which is often too late.

The other source of energy is that supplied by humans and this source is used much more than that of animals. The tasks performed by humans are few and quite similar in this society as compared with an industrialized one. Because of this, there is a correspondingly greater degree of substitutability of workers for these tasks. All are farmers first, so any adult can be hired for the various tasks related to raising corn and beans. To increase the output of work more laborers are added instead of attempting to organize the task that they are performing. Actually most of the tasks that are performed are unorganizable so that if a man wants to get his cornfield hoed sooner than he can do it by himself, he hires people to help him. They necessarily all do the same thing together.

There are times, though, when organizing the task would be more efficient but this is not done. In the case of building the airstrip, for example, there were only a limited number of people who had picks, bars, and shovels. The rest only had their hoes to use, which were intended for hoeing corn and not for digging or moving dirt. It would have been a better use of labor, in my opinion, if crews had been set up with a proportionate amount of the scarce tools divided among them. But that is not the way the authorities organized the task. Everyone, everyday, was supposed to work regardless of the tools available to the task.

It is true that everyone is a farmer in this village, but some are also carpenters, tile and brick makers, lime makers, net makers, and seamstresses in their spare time. The skills involved in these tasks are passed on from parent to child and guarded jealously. There is the belief that a man should not teach anyone else his trade because then the apprentice would know more

The wooden whorl is spun by hand to twist strands of string together to make cord.

than the master since he will know not only what the master taught him but also what he brought to the learning situation.

The economic position of everyone in this situation is precarious because of low crop yields and the small capital investment required to be a farmer or any other craftsman. Starving is a real possibility since there is no surplus to speak of that can be stored from a good year to take care of a person's needs during a bad year. Years are good or bad depending on the amount and timing of the rains and the collective anxiety of the group is expressed in talk about when it is going to rain again.

Bugs make the storing of grain a serious problem. They attack corn and beans while they are maturing and by the time the farmer stores his grain, the bug population is well entrenched. They effectively reduce corn to powder and riddle beans with holes. The only native treatment for this problem is to dig a hole in the ground and build a fire on top of rocks that have been placed in the hole. Then, the ears of corn with their shucks still intact are piled on top of the heated rocks and the hole is covered up with dirt. This oven treatment kills the bugs that are causing the damage and keeps this part of the crop at least intact for human consumption. But this method is not widely used because the Chontals feel that it ruins the good taste of the corn.

A bad year is a disaser because no one has enough corn left over from the previous year. When the rains fail, and each year produces its anxious

Cord is woven into nets that are used to catch fish and shrimp.

moments, the ones who can leave, do, and seek work someplace else so that they can buy corn. The price of corn almost doubles in a bad year while wages stay the same so that their predicament is compounded. Those who cannot leave exist on the generosity of friends and relatives and supplement their diet with edible wild plants. The really bad years are never forgotten and are used as a standard to measure other years that are only bad.

DIVISION OF LABOR

The division of labor in this economy follows the axes of sex and age but there are many tasks that both sexes do. Both sexes carry water, plant, weed, harvest crops, carry loads, cut wood, and take animals to graze. The men, though, usually do any work that involves the use of an axe, because of the strength required, so they do the initial clearing of a field. They are the only ones who make adobes, bricks, tiles, lime, and mescal. They are also the only carpenters and house builders. Women wash clothes, keep house, prepare the family food, and care for the young. Both sexes enter into these tasks in their early teens or before and continue, to some extent, until they die. Disengagement begins when their health does not permit them to work at the heavier tasks but they keep at the less physically demanding jobs as long as they are able.

There is a type of solidarity present in this economy that is not due to the occupational dependence of one person on another as is true of a modern economy where one person is paid to do his specialty and someone else is paid to do his. Instead, the solidarity in this society comes from the workers having the same cognitive mapping of the world. The integration that is present is through shared concepts that each has. They all believe that God intended for them to be busy at work and they are, even if this involves acting busy. Some are busier than others, but no one spends sober days in leisure when the rest of the village is working. The standard reply of a wife to the question of whether her husband is home or not is that he has his work and is doing it.

The productive units in this economy are derivative from the other social units of the society. A man tends to hire relatives for a task that requires help rather than nonrelatives who might be more efficient hoers or field clearers. He will also be more likely to hire people from his own barrio rather than from the other one so that social group regulations enter into every group task. The productive units then are not economically purposed but are more multipurposed. If a man owes a debt to someone else, he may work it off and be included in the group of people hired to hoe corn. Debtors and relatives present possible role conflict situations since they may have more prestige in the community than the man who hired them. He has to take this into consideration when working with them and cannot treat them in strictly an employer–employee relationship. One of the women in the group may have a small child that she has to bring with her and nurse from time to time, stopping her hoeing to meet his needs.

The worst kind of a life for a Chontal would be to live strictly as a hired man. He is paid only 4 pesos a day (32 cents) and furnished with two meals. He has to provide his own hoe which can cost him up to 20 pesos, or his own machete or axe which costs 25 and 40 pesos apiece. The money he makes will only buy enough corn to feed a large family for one day. In the process of earning this money, he is wearing out both his hoe and the clothing that he wears. If he wants to work without meals furnished by his employer, he is paid 8 pesos a day. The day begins at seven in the morning and does not end until six at night, filled with some of the most monotonous work that I have ever done.

LAND TENURE

Land is owned either by private individuals or by the village. Private land is bought and sold through a written deed in Spanish that follows a standard form having six parts. This deed is drawn up by the secretary of the alcalde who is paid up to 10 pesos for his work, and it is signed by the alcalde for a fee of 5 pesos. Two witnesses are required to sign the deed and they are paid several pesos each. The whole transaction costs about 20 pesos and some buyers are reluctant to add this cost on to the purchase of the land which may have only cost them 100 pesos. In that case they pay the seller the price of the land and he surrenders his deed to the buyer without a new one being drawn up. The community recognizes the transaction as a valid one even though it is not recorded in writing. This may be due to the fact that the deed is written in language that is not understood and all that is required is that the two parties involved, buyer and seller, be satisfied.

Neither land nor houses are rented partly because the parties involved do not want to draw up such a contract. We did rent half of the house that belonged to a man whom I refer to as our landlord in this book. We began paying him 25 pesos a month but he was never comfortable accepting our money and as soon as he saw that we were putting improvements into his house, he refused to accept any more money. Then, too, there is enough village land that citizens are free to use as long as they pay their annual contribution that goes into a fund to purchase wax for making fiesta candles. This village land tends to be located farther from the village than private land and some of it is claimed by other individuals or other villages so that it has disadvantages associated with it. If a person continues to farm a piece of village land it is considered as his property and can be passed on to his descendants. It can never be sold, though, and once the owner leaves the village for any extended period of time, someone else can claim the land.

Private land is passed on to the wife of the deceased if she has children; if not, the property goes to the brothers of the deceased but not to his sisters. This practice was brought rather forcefully to our attention when our landlord was shot during the land dispute with Santa Lucía. His brother, who was a disgrace to him because he begged for money on the streets of Tehuantepec, heard that our landlord had been shot and perhaps killed. He returned to the village to see if the report was true, and if so, to dispossess our landlady of her house and property. The landlord and his wife were childless and the only way to pass the property on to her in the event of his death would have been for them to go to San Carlos and become legally married. As it is now, they and every other married couple in the village are listed in the government records as being single.

This lack of government recognition for couples who live together by consent, or have been married by the village authorities and the priest, is a source of conflict to them. I heard one former villager who returned for a brief visit tell his relatives that they lived like hogs since they were not legally married. In another instance, a man whose wife had died, took her sister as his wife to help him raise his children. When his boys reached adulthood, they were able to get a document signed by authorities outside the village deeding their deceased mother's property to them. They then presented the document to the village officials who had no choice but to evict the man and his wife.

The boys left town as soon as they had evicted their father and stepmother and the property now sits empty.

PLANTS AND AGRICULTURE

The Chontal people have an extensive knowledge of both wild and domesticated plants. What is presented here is especially sketchy of wild plants with a fuller treatment of domesticated plants. Wild plants are used for food, medicine, and miscellaneous purposes. The most important wild foods are tomatoes, chipile, and cactus. The leaves of the chipile plant, which resemble alfalfa, are cooked and used as a tortilla dip. Cactus leaves, once the thorns have been scraped off, are cut into thin strips and cooked in water or with some other food. They taste like, and have the appearance of, green beans.

Medicinal plants are used to lower a fever, cure a cough, reduce swelling, heal skin rashes and wounds, plus other less defined symptoms. The most dramatic treatment uses a poisonous weed called Córdoba. Three drops of the sap from this weed are placed in a glass of water and drunk. The sick person vomits immediately and it is believed that whatever is causing his sickness is expelled. Some people know more about the medicinal value of wild plants than others and a few of them will only share this knowledge if they are paid a fee. The fees range up to 25 pesos which struck me as high since the medicine does not cost anything. Cures are effected through the use of some of these medicinal plants while the curative powers of other plants are questionable. A complicating factor is that a person might have the same symptoms as someone else who was helped through a medicinal wild plant but have quite a different ailment.

The most important plants in the miscellaneous category would be trees, vines, and grass. Trees are the only source of fuel for domestic cooking and the processing of mescal, bricks, tile, and lime. Oak is used for cooking because of its long-burning characteristics while pine is used for other fires where a hot fire of shorter duration is suitable. Small forked oak trees are used for corner posts in building a house while the straighter and lighter pine poles are used for the roof. Boards for the door of the house, benches, tables, and chairs are ripped out of the trunk of a large pine or cedar tree. Vines are used in making a grass roof to tie the clumps of grass to the horizontal bamboo poles. These poles are tied to vertical pine poles which in turn are tied to a roof pole. The grass that is used for roofs is a variety that grows especially long and is found at a distance from the village.

The most important domestic plant by far is corn and it is the only source of food that has an origin myth:

> Some people saw that an ant had a kernel of corn so they asked him where he got it. He refused to tell so they seized him and tied a rope around his stomach so tight that it almost cut him in two (this is why the ant's stomach is so narrow in one place). They followed him to a huge rock where he told them to untie him so that he could go underneath the rock. The ant was gone for an hour and when he came back up again he was carrying a kernel of corn. He told them if they

would break the rock apart, they would find a lot more corn. So the people went and asked a thunder god to strike the rock with lightning and see if the ant was telling the truth. If he was lying, they intended to kill him and they had him tied up again. The thunder god struck the rock with lightning but nothing happened. So the people asked another thunder god whose name was Crippled Thunder God to strike the rock with lightning. As soon as he did, a big pile of corn was uncovered. The people told the ant that he could have whatever kernels were dropped and they began to gather the corn together. The Crippled Thunder God told the people that there were two types of corn present. The big ears of corn would require six month's growing season and the little ears of corn would only require three. He also told them that they should let the ant go free and allow him to eat whatever corn he wanted since he was the one who first showed them where the corn was.

There are two types of corn, three- and six-month; both types require the same kind of care. The initial planting of a field is preceded by cutting down trees and undergrowth that are allowed to dry out during the months of December through May when no rainfall of any consequence falls in this region. The field is set on fire starting at the bottom or lower part of the field since it is almost always located on a mountain slope. The fire burns up the slope with enough heat to reduce the undergrowth to ashes and destroy some of the bug population. The larger tree trunks that have been felled do not burn and are used either for firewood or for lumber. The field is planted as soon as the rainy season begins, usually the end of May or the beginning of June. Planting is done with a dibble stick which may be nothing more than a pole sharpened with a tapered end or tipped with a worn-out metal hoe blade. The seeds are carried in a hollowed-out gourd that is strapped around the waist. In the gourd will be squash and bean seed along with the kernels of corn to be planted. Three or four seeds taken at random are placed in each hole made by the dibble stick. These holes are spaced from 3 to 5 feet apart depending on the quality of the soil and the slope of the hill. The beans will ripen first with the corn and squash being harvested much later.

Corn is attacked in a variety of ways, starting with the green shoot that breaks through the surface of the ground. Road-runner birds and other large birds pull up the shoot to eat the still largely intact kernel on the other end. These birds can be destructive enough that parts of the cornfield may have to be replanted. Once the corn plant gets beyond this stage it is threatened more by drought than any factor.

The two different varieties of corn that the villager plants are a kind of insurance against drought. The three-month variety is planted at the river on the slopes of the foothills in sandy soil. It grows fast during the hot days and nights and will produce a good crop if it gets the early rain at crucial intervals, especially when the ears are forming. Because of the heat and the sandy soil, though, it is seriously damaged by any extended dry period. The six-month variety is planted at a higher elevation in loam or clay soil near the village. This soil holds the moisture better than the sandy soil of the river. The nights are always cool near the village so that this corn can withstand more drought than the three-month corn. If this longer growing corn gets the late rains it can recover to a certain extent from early drought conditions. Almost never does one crop fail completely, but there are many years when one or the other has its yield reduced because of the lack of timely rains.

Corn is hoed twice during its growing season with the first year's sowing less affected by weeds than the following years. A piece of cleared land is only sown for four years because of the loss of fertility due to the erosion of cleared land. Then, too, the weeds come back stronger each year. After four years of crops the field is abandoned for four to eight years. During this time the soil's fertility is at least partially restored through natural growth processes before the field is used again.

When the corn is ready to tassel out it may be damaged by high winds that blow the stalks over and reduce the crop yield. Once the corn is in its milk stage it has to be protected against raccoons, foxes, and skunks. Either the owner camps out at night in his field with his dogs or ties them at various places in his field to scare off these animals. As the corn begins to dry in the ear, the only threat left is the damage done by bugs which has been discussed earlier. It may sound as if corn is not a dependable food source because of all the problems mentioned above. Actually, corn is the most dependable food crop grown by the Chontals because the other crops face even more serious threats from leaf-eating insects.

Corn, however, is not a good money crop for the people of San Matías. A field 150 yards square will yield a crop in a good year that will sell for 150 pesos. But there will be twenty-four days of labor involved in growing the corn: three days clearing the field, one day planting; eighteen days hoeing; and two days of harvesting. The man's profit for this crop is almost nothing beyond the 8 pesos a day wages that he could have been earning if he had been working for someone else. But then of course he would not want to work for someone else for that length of time nor would anyone hire him for that extended period of time.

The people of Zapotitlán do much better with corn as a cash crop. Their fields are more fertile and their rain supply is much more dependable. The same size field near Zapotitlán will produce one and a half to two times as much corn as a field near San Matías. Even when corn crops fail elsewhere, driving up the price of corn, the people of Zapotitlán have corn to sell. Their village and fields are located just to the north of a ridge of mountains where the rain clouds from the ocean drop their rain as they continue to move inland.

Corn is considered to be especially delicious when it is in the roasting ear stage. After the kernels have passed this stage and are hardened, they are softened through boiling in lime water and a number of different kinds of food are prepared from them. Tortillas are the most important food made from corn and are formed into the size of a small pizza. Since the better tasting tortillas are thin, there is quite an art involved in patting them out without the tortilla falling apart. Atole is made from grinding up the softened corn kernels. The corn dough can then be mixed with water and eaten raw or cooked in water, like mush, and served as a thick gruel. Raw corn dough is the main ingredient in tamales and sometimes is rolled into baseball-size balls that are roasted in the fire. By any standard of measure, corn is the most versatile and important source of food that the Chontals have.

Beans are next in importance to corn and they are planted along with it, as well as in separate plots. When beans are planted separately, they are planted during the last week in June. Beans are less adaptable than corn and cannot be planted in clay soil. The people also believe that some plots of land are more troubled with bugs than others and these are not used as bean fields. Bean plants are eaten by bugs to a far greater extent than corn and sometimes the damage wipes out most or all of the potential crop. There are pesticides that would kill these bugs or at least prevent them from eating the beans, but no one uses pesticides. These people would not know which pesticide to buy or where to buy it. Even if they did, the cash value of the crop would not make it economically feasible to buy pesticides. Beans are an important source of protein and it is unfortunate that they are subject to such bug damage. A dry quart measure of beans sells for about 3 pesos, more than twice the price of

Planting corn in a piece of ground with a dibble stick. The tree limbs in the foreground were not burned when the field was set on fire.

corn, and more than most people can afford to buy. But beans are still cheaper than meat and are used as a meat substitute for some fiestas. Both varieties of bean are black. One variety is boiled in water with lard and seasoning added until it turns to gruel; the other variety retains its shape no matter how long it is cooked. Beans are also eaten in their pods when they are in the green bean stage, cooked in water with lard.

The next most important domesticated food would be the several varieties of squash that are grown. There is a type of pumpkin squash that is raised as well as a squash that has white flesh. Both are cut into chunks and boiled in water before they are eaten.

There are a variety of other vegetables eaten by the Chontals but only one more, red chili peppers, will be mentioned here because of its economic importance. They are grown in quantity by the people of San Matías to sell to people in neighboring villages. Chili plants are less affected by drought than corn and give the best cash return for time and money invested. The same size cornfield that yielded almost no profit, beyond paying the man his wages, when planted in chili peppers would ideally net him a profit of over 3000 pesos. But, unlike corn which can be planted for four years in the same field, chili pepper plants can only be raised for one year on cleared ground because of the weed problem. One man found it profitable to raise only chili peppers and sell them as a cash crop. He used part of the profit to buy corn and other food. He is the only man that I know of who did not depend on growing corn for his own needs. Most people who raise chili peppers do it on a smaller scale and sell their dried peppers at the biggest fiesta in the region, the fiesta of Santo Domingo held in that village on the eighth of December.

Fruit is seldom sold among the Chontals but is eaten by the family of the grower or given to friends who stop by to visit. Peaches, which are quite scarce, are an exception, but even they are given away to visitors. From a food standpoint, bananas would be the most important source of nourishment with four quite different varieties grown. Next in importance would be avocados and mangos, with oranges, lemon-limes, and lemons of less importance. Leaf-cutter ants often damage citrus trees so much that no crop of fruit can be produced. Fortunately these ants do not bother the other fruit-bearing trees to this extent.

Sugar cane is raised by everyone who has a plot of land along the river that can be irrigated. The stalks are cut into two-foot pieces and, after the outer covering is stripped off, they are chewed on for their sugar water content by people as they walk along the trail. Once a year, the crop is cut down and processed into brown sugar. The heaviest work is squeezing the sugar water out of the cane and this is done by a homemade wooden press that may be small enough to be turned by two men or big enough to require the use of a pair of oxen.

Both presses are made completely of wood, even to the gears of the large press. As the oxen turn the center cylinder, its teeth catch in slots in the outer two cylinders and turn them. A man feeds the sugar cane between the revolving cylinders and the sugar water is then caught in a large metal tub. The

An elderly woman shaping corn dough into a tortilla. The small stone (mano de metate) resting in the large stone (metate) was used to grind up the corn into dough of the proper consistency to shape.

tub when filled is placed over a fire and the sugar water is cooked with a little bit of ash water until it begins to thicken. It is taken off the fire and stirred until it is ready to be poured into molds in a wooden beam. As it cools it becomes a solid cake of brown sugar about the size of a cereal bowl and it sells for 2½ pesos. Here again, the same amount of ground that yielded no net profit in corn would yield ideally a net profit of over 1000 pesos if planted in sugar cane for a year. But irrigated river land is scarce and no one owns much of it.

The cash crop that most Chontals depend on is mescal. It is processed from the maguey or century plant that requires eight years to mature. However, corn can be planted in the same field with the maguey plants for five of those eight years. When the plants are mature, the leaves are cut off and may be used in making rope. The base of the plant is cut off from the root and sectioned into chunks that are carried away to an oven site. The oven is a hole dug about 4 feet deep in the ground with a diameter of about 8 feet. Rocks are put in the bottom of this oven and a pile of wood is set on fire on top of the rocks. When the fire has gone out, the chunks of maguey plant are placed on the rocks and stacked up a few feet above ground level. Then grass is laid over the maguey chunks and dirt is thrown on top of the grass to help hold the heat in the oven. A pole that was placed in the center of the oven before the maguey chunks were stacked up is now removed and water is poured down the hole left by the pole. The steam that results from the water reaching the hot rocks is then trapped in the oven and helps to bake the maguey.

When the maguey is considered to be properly baked, the chunks are laid out on the ground to cool off. Little pieces of cooked maguey can be eaten at this stage. Actually only the flesh between the fibers is eaten; it is quite sweet and tastes like licorice. The chunks are then carried to the distillery site and mashed up in a trough by a man using what looks like a large baseball bat. The mashed-up maguey is put into a squeezer made of maguey rope woven on the bias. As a man twists this around a pole, the maguey juice is squeezed into a wooden vat and the fiber thrown away. The juice is allowed to ferment and bubble until it reaches a certain stage. Then, following the traditional method, it is cooked in a series of pots set into a stove made of dried mud. A pot without a bottom rests on the top of each of the cooking pots and the vapor from the cooking fermented juice rises into this pot chamber where condensation takes place as it comes in contact with the bottom of a metal dipper. These metal dippers are the only metal used in the whole process and they have water running through them constantly to keep them cool. At the bottom of each dipper is a maguey leaf that catches the condensation and channels it into a hollowed-out piece of bamboo which in turn has a string on the end of it. The distilled mescal drops off the end of the string into a pottery container. The mescal at this stage is not considered strong enough so it is distilled once more before it is ready to be drunk or sold. Most of the mescal made in San Matías is sold to men from other towns who have pack animals and who make frequent trips to Huamelula where mescal is bought in quantity. Mescal contains enough alcohol for a pint of it to make a man drunk. Here once again, the same amount of ground that yielded no net profit in corn would yield ideally a net profit of about 1000 pesos. But this profit would be spread over eight years and would not be realized unless corn were planted in the same maguey field for five of the eight years.

LIVESTOCK, HUNTING, AND TRADE

In addition to the pack animals and oxen mentioned above, the Chontals also raise chickens, turkeys, and hogs. Turkeys are difficult for these people to raise and are usually sold to traders rather than eaten. Chickens are much easier to raise than turkeys and their eggs provide a small but important source of income. Eggs can be bought three for a peso in the village and then sold two for a peso or slightly higher in the valley town of Tequisistlán. But chickens are subject to epidemic disease that sweeps through the village every few years and almost wipes out the entire chicken population. This results in quite a loss since each grown chicken is worth from 12 to 15 pesos.

Hogs are raised by the owner of a sow entering into partnerships with individuals who feed the young and take care of them until they are ready to be butchered. Then, the profits are divided equally among the owner and the one who raised the animal. Hogs are not subject to epidemic diseases nor are they affected by paralytic rabies, even though bitten by infected bats. The layer of fat that a hog has under his skin seems to act as a barrier to the spread of

An ox-driven sugar cane press. Note that no metal is used in this machine; even the gears are wooden.

the disease. The biggest threat to hogs is worm infestation, which usually only slows down the growing and fattening process but can, in extreme cases, result in the death of the animal. Hogs take more than twice as long to mature and fatten in San Matías as they do in my home state of Illinois. Poor nutrition and worm infestation are certainly the main factors contributing to slow growth, but inbreeding is also responsible. The owner of a sow will not keep a good boar just for breeding purposes nor will anyone else. He breeds his sow with one of her offspring who is just barely big enough to service her, and then the owner castrates him and the other males in the litter. This inbreeding results in small litters of three or four pigs of inferior stock. Pork is sold, as is beef, in strips as thick as a man's thumb and twice as long as the span between the end of his index finger and thumb when spread apart. These strips cost a peso each.

A number of wild animals exists in these mountains including wild hogs, deer, porcupines, armadillos, rabbits, and squirrels, but none of them is a dependable source of meat. There is a scarcity of game since open season is the rule all year long and both females and the young are killed along with the adult males. Deer meat is valued, in my opinion, not because it tastes any better than, or even as good as, other meat, but because there is a certain amount of prestige associated with killing such a large animal.

Fishing is not any more dependable a source of food than wild game basically for the same reasons. The use of nets and dynamite blasting has decimated the fish population. Then, too, it is reported that government DDT sprayers have killed large quantities of fish by rinsing their spray tanks in the river.

The Chontals sell to outsiders such items as mescal, chili peppers, hogs, turkeys, chickens, eggs, and hides. They are either too far from markets to sell their mangos, avocados, and bananas, or unwilling to attempt it. They buy from outsiders everything that they own made of metal: axes, hoes, machetes, saws, hammers, knives, picks, shovels, bars, lanterns, tubs, dippers, grinders, sewing machines, guns, and flashlights. They buy either the cloth out of which to make clothing or the clothing itself. They also buy transistor radios, hand victrolas, blankets, morrals or carrying bags, and huaraches. They have been particularly hard hit by inflation with some items increasing in cost at the rate of 5 percent a year while what the Chontal has to sell has not kept pace. Nor have his wages kept up with prices in the last ten years. At 8 pesos a day, he has to work seven days to buy a pair of pants and a shirt; six days for a grinder; five days for a large tub; four days for an axe head, machete, digging bar, pick, or hammer; three days for a shovel, bucket, or flashlight; two days for a hoe head; and almost one day for a set of batteries for a flashlight. The bigger items are at the limits of his resources: 600 pesos for a radio, 500 pesos for a gun, and 400 pesos for a victrola.

WEALTH DIFFERENCES

Although these mountain people live in the type of an economy that does not produce large surpluses, they are very much conscious of wealth differences. The types of houses discussed above are an example of this and there is the desire on the part of most everyone to live in the most expensive type of house. The type of clothing that an individual wears to a fiesta reflects his wealth, especially his hat, jacket, and shoes. Radios have for the most part replaced victrolas as prestige items to own, and almost every family in San Matías has one.

These wealth differences have not been eliminated through the sociocultural conflicts that are supposed to operate in this type of society: fiestas, witchcraft, and banditry. All three are present but none of them prevents people from attempting to accumulate and display more wealth than someone else.

A Chontal woman with her tump-line carrying a chunk of the base of a maguey plant. This chunk, which may weigh up to 50 pounds, is being carried to an earth oven.

3

Cultural System

THE CULTURE OF A GROUP of people can be thought of as a model of and for reality. It selects and emphasizes only certain beliefs from an almost infinite number of possibilities. These beliefs in turn influence the group's perception of life. If separate groups of people never come into contact with other groups of people, then each would probably continue to perceive life only in terms of its own belief system. It is doubtful whether people would even be aware of their own beliefs if they were not exposed to the contrasting views of other groups of people. The Chontals have had varying degrees of contact with the culture of Spanish speakers for perhaps 400 years. These mountain people have both accepted and rejected certain aspects of the larger Mexican culture. What they have accepted has almost always been modified so that it would have a better fit with the rest of their culture. At times the cultural aspect that has been borrowed has been modified so much that it would be difficult, if not impossible, to say what is Chontal and what is Spanish. This is especially true of the language spoken by these people, which contains words of Spanish origin.

Language

The consensus of opinion among linguists is that Chontal is a member of the Hokan phylum of languages, which is spread out through parts of California, Arizona, Baja California, northwestern Mexico, northeastern Mexico, southeastern Mexico, Honduras, and Nicaragua.

There are two Chontal languages in Oaxaca that are obviously related: Highland and Lowland. The Highland language is the more conservative of the two and has changed less from the original language. Highland and Lowland Chontal are called separate languages because speakers from each language use Spanish in communicating with each other instead of their own native language. A comparison of 200 words that are used by linguists to determine

56

whether languages are related or not showed that 70 percent of these words appear to be related. Of these related words between the two languages, 20 percent sound exactly alike. A speaker of one language listening to the other language can understand the related words just enough that the different sounds produce an interference with his own language. The words that are not related at all keep him from understanding what is being communicated. The Lowland Chontals are much more bilingual than the Highland group and many of the younger people cannot speak Chontal at all. To be able to speak Chontal is a prestige factor because only the older ones are fluent in this language. The reverse is true in the Highland area where Spanish is the prestige language and only a few can speak it fluently.

In both areas children are spoken to in Spanish and they learn it before they learn Chontal. The kind of Spanish they learn follows some of the rules of Chontal pronunciation and grammar so that they can later begin speaking their native language with a minimum of adjustment. Children continue speaking Spanish up until they are in their early twenties. Then, if they live in the Highland area, they begin to speak Chontal, probably because their dealings with older adults require it. But until this time, a conversation between an adolescent and an adult is often characterized by the use of two languages. The adolescent understands Chontal but responds in Spanish. They do not use the same language in speaking to each other because they are both not sure enough of their speaking knowledge of that language. The type of Spanish spoken is impoverished both in grammar and in the more abstract concepts so that it is not adequate for all of life's experiences. And since it is easier and more culturally appropriate for the young to adapt themselves to the language of their elders, most of them switch over to Chontal and only speak Spanish with their peers or younger children.

There are a few instances in which an individual will refuse to make the adjustment and continue to speak Spanish for the rest of his life. This situation is apt to occur in a more bilingual village but there is one woman in San Matías who never responds to other villagers in Chontal. She does speak Chontal to us, though, so that it is not a matter of inability on her part to learn the language. Chontal is difficult to learn, however, because of the many irregularities in its grammar. She was laughed at for the mistakes she made when she began to speak Chontal. She was so embarrassed that she decided to continue speaking Spanish and not make the change. No one laughs at her Spanish, although it, too, contains mistakes, because no one knows Spanish well enough to correct her. But she does speak Chontal to us since, as she told us, we do not laugh at her mistakes.

The Chontals for the most part do not take pride in their language. They are unlike the Zapotecans of Mexico who not only speak good Spanish but are fluent in their native language. A Chontal will speak either Spanish or Chontal but hardly any of the mountain people will master both languages. The largest village in the area, Ecatepec, has only a few speakers left who speak Chontal. Those who do are ashamed of their language and will attempt to conceal it from Spanish speakers.

My attempts at speaking their language have met with a mixed response depending on the context in which it was spoken. If all the people present spoke Chontal, then they were pleased that I could converse with them. If, on the other hand, there were Spanish speakers present from the outside world, then some of the mountain people were embarrassed if I used Chontal. Once I attended a village meeting in which a school official from Oaxaca was being honored. He and three other speakers, all outsiders, emphasized the need for the school in the community. Then I was called upon to say something and, after a few introductory remarks in Spanish, I began speaking in Chontal so that the villagers would better understand what I was saying. The speakers who preceded me reacted favorably to my use of Chontal in this situation but I could sense that some of the villagers were uneasy, especially the young people.

Our experience in teaching them to read their own language first, which they can understand, and Spanish later, has been disappointing. They are motivated only to learn to read Spanish, which they cannot understand because they lack the necessary vocabulary and grammar. In this situation their language is maladaptive. It is maladaptive because of their own feelings of inferiority toward it, not because of any inherent deficiency in the language. Their language could be used to help them understand Spanish but it is not utilized due to their lack of interest in written Chontal. Instead of their language being a social flag around which they could unite as a group, it seems to remind them of their own inadequacies.

Ideology

The Chontals use the same reasoning processes as we do and yet they arrive at quite different conclusions. This is because they start off with different propositions than we do, not because there is anything deficient in their reasoning. The ancient syllogism, "all men are mortal; Socrates is a man; therefore Socrates is mortal" is accepted by us because we recognize that any proposition that is valid for a class is valid for any member of that class. The Chontals, in a less formal but similar manner, reason that, "Witches can harm people; Juan is a witch; therefore Juan can harm people." This type of reasoning is correct, given acceptance of the first two propositions. It is the propositions, then, of the Chontals that are responsible for their different conclusions about life. This section will describe some of the basic propositions that they use in arriving at conclusions.

WORLD VIEW

The Chontal does not make the kind of sharp distinctions that we make between personal and impersonal forces in the world. Their distinction between humans and animals is not as sharp as ours nor do they differentiate to the extent that we do between animal and plant kingdoms. Chontals feel more of a kinship tie with the world and everything in it than we do. This results in a more passive approach to life that contrasts with the active attempt of Americans to master life's problems. For example, the Chontal believes that the wind is alive and can be offended in ways similar to offending a human being. Mountains are alive and are populated by little people who appear and disappear in whimsical fashion. Human-like beings also live in the river and are responsible at times for abducting people in mysterious ways.

The Chontal does not look to a far off God to meet his needs as much as he does to what is immediately present in his world. There are several stories that relate how God tried to do something and failed so that he is not the omnipotent and omniscient person of Christian belief. In one story he tried to make it rain on earth three times but never succeeded in soaking the soil. So he turned the task over to the mountains and they were able to get the job done where he had failed.

These mountain people see human forms in cumulus clouds and consider them to be gods that are responsible for the dark rain-bearing clouds and lightning. There is a story that tells how a man was swallowed by an alligator and taken to the land of the rain gods. There he saw how they waved black pieces of cloth around to form the rain clouds. He saw how they swung their machetes and caused lightning to flash and thunder to roll. He was brought back to earth and warned not to tell where he had been and what he had seen. As long as he kept his secret his crops never failed for lack of rain. But he finally told his secret and he lost the favor that he had enjoyed with the rain gods.

The lack of sharp distinction between humans and animals can be seen in both their behavior and in their stories. Any animal that is fatally sick or injured is never put out of his misery but is left alone to die. My impression is that they would consider it just as wrong to put an animal out of his misery as we would to practice mercy killing of hopelessly sick or injured humans.

There often is a special bond between a man and a particular animal such as a lion or tiger that is thought to be his *nahual* or animal counterpart. If someone insults him or injures him in any way, his animal counterpart will avenge him by killing the other man's livestock. The fate of the man and the animal are considered to be closely tied together so that what affects one affects the other.

In addition to the special relationship between people and their animal counterparts, there is also a strong bond between humans and dogs. In one of their creation myths that involves a flood, one man is saved because of a type of ark that he built. After he emerged from his ark, he disobeyed one of God's commands and was turned into a dog.

These people also refer to the devil as the older brother who, in some ways at least, is smarter than God. According to another one of their creation myths, God made the first man and woman without sex organs. The devil realized that they could never reproduce that way so he supplied them with sex organs. He cut off his own lips for the woman's sex organ and after failing to stick them in her armpit or behind her knee he finally succeeded in sticking them between her legs. After he made a penis for the man, the devil showed the two of them how to have intercourse. As soon as they had intercourse, man and his wife were driven out of the garden for their sin. They sinned in having intercourse because God intended for them to reproduce in some other way, perhaps like fruit growing on a tree. Here again there is not as sharp a distinction between the devil and God as is found in Christianity, and man's original sin is such that he can hardly be held accountable for it.

The Chontal is conscious of the fact that he works harder than outsiders and makes less money. He realizes that outsiders make their money through "white collar jobs" rather than sweating in the field. He has feelings of inferiority because of his position in relation to these outsiders and he attributes part of the discrepancy to his inability to read or write. The rest of the responsibility for his unenviable position is placed on his patron deity who refused to do what he was told. According to the account, as soon as Christ was born, the Virgin Mary told the patron deity of the Chontals to roll in the afterbirth. He refused to do it because it made him sick to his stomach. She told him that if he had done what she told him to do, the Chontals would not have to work so hard for the things that they wanted. They would have been rich. Just then the patron saint of the foreigners came and was told to do the same thing. Immediately he rolled in the afterbirth and Mary said that the foreigners would not have to work hard for their living.

DISEASE

These people either do not know or do not understand the concept of sickness caused by germs. They have remedies and medicinal herbs that they use to treat the symptoms of diseases, but, if the treatment is not satisfactory, they call on the local curer. I asked a young man once to describe what is said and done when someone visits the curer. He gave me the following account:

Patient: Good day, Uncle. We have come because we are sick. Can you treat us?
Curer: What is your sickness?
P: We have a headache. What medicine should we take?
C: I can treat you if you have brought what is needed.
P: What is needed?
C: Well, either copal (resin that is burned) or an egg.
P: Oh, an egg? We brought an egg. (It had been rubbed all over the body of the sick person.)
C: Well, then I will treat you. Who is sick? This one who came with you?
P: The one who is sick did not come but can't we call him?
C: Do you want me to call him right away or tomorrow?
P: We want you to call him now.
  The curer takes a piece of broken pottery or tortilla griddle and burns copal in it. He then waves the incense around while spraying water out of his mouth in a fine mist. As he does this he calls the name of the sick person and tells him to get up, and he also tells the spirit of the ground or mountain to let the spirit of the sick person go free. The curer does this because the sick person might have become frightened and lost his spirit to the mountain. Then the curer gathers together a little pile of dirt that the people brought with them perhaps from the spot where they thought the sick person was frightened. The curer

puts copal on top of the dirt and then places the egg on the copal. He lights the copal on fire and calls the sick person again by spraying out water from his mouth. If the egg explodes and puts out the fire, he says that the sick person will recover. If the egg, on the other hand, does not explode he tells them that the sick person was not frightened but has a different type of sickness. Then he consults his oracle book to see what sickness it is. He tells them that someone is jealous of the sick person, or made fun of the sick person, or is using witchcraft against the sick person, and that is why he is sick. The curer asks them who is doing this and they can usually remember someone who might be guilty. They pay the curer about 20 pesos and leave. If the sick person does not get well and they return to the curer, he will tell them that the disease has gone too far. They should have come at the start of the sickness and there is nothing more that he can do.

The curer, who has just recently died, was the oldest man in the village and his reputation for being able to diagnose the ailments of people and cure them was known throughout the Chontal region. However, when I asked him to tell me about his techniques, he maintained that he knew almost nothing about curing people. He was willing to give me any other information that I asked him for, but, until just before his death, he refused to talk to me about curing ceremonies. He used to ask me, when I persisted in my request, that if he really knew anything about medicine and curing people, then why did his wife die from illness? The question seemed like a good one to us, but obviously neither he nor his people took it seriously because he continued to treat people who sought him out. Once when I was tape recording material from him at his ranch, two men arrived from a neighboring village. They did not state their business until after I had left but it is common knowledge that people came from all over this mountain area to consult with the old man. If one of his own people had asked him the question that he posed to me, he would have had an answer for it. He would have said that his wife, as well as any patients of his who did not recover, died because it was not their destiny to live a long time. That kind of reasoning is accepted by the Chontals who, in their passive attitude toward life, accept their ultimate disappointments with fatalistic resignation.

When it seemed that the old man had effected a cure, the person who was sick told others of the curer's power. In this way those who already believed in the curer had their confidence confirmed. Those who were not sure of his ability had their doubts satisfied, and those who did not believe in him at all, began to wonder if there was not something to it after all.

The old man was confident enough to practice his cures openly in the daytime even though his curing technique was enough like witchcraft that the two could be mistaken. However, he claimed that he was not a witch and his work instead was to cure people, not to make them sick. Most of the villagers believed him.

WITCHCRAFT

One of the last aspects of the cultural system of a group of people that is discovered and investigated by the anthropologist is witchcraft. This was our experience also since we lived in this village for several years before we were aware of the extent to which witchcraft was practiced. The first time that I heard something suspicious was when a young man from San Matías was relating an incident to me. We were in Mitla and I was tape recording text material for linguistic analysis when he used a word that I had never heard before. The incident that he was relating was about a woman who had died giving birth to twins. She was able to give birth to one of the twins but not the other. The midwife pulled the other twin from her and in the process must have damaged the mother internally. Some of her insides came with the baby and she soon died of a massive infection. When her husband saw what came with the baby he was convinced that she was the victim of witchcraft. He believed that someone had put the insides of a deer into his wife through witchcraft and this was what was expelled with the baby.

When I questioned the young man giving me the account why anyone would put such an object into another person, he replied that someone must have wanted deer meat from the deceased. When her husband killed a deer someone might have asked her to sell some and she refused to either sell or give any of it away. The dissatisfied person then got his revenge through witchcraft. He placed in her body what she had refused to sell him. This was the first time that anyone had told me that this woman died from other than natural causes. But the incident also helped to explain another puzzling word that can be translated as "force."

A number of times individuals had told me that they did not want to do something but they did it because of "force." In one instance I had bought shotgun shells for a man and later when I asked him about them he told me that they were all gone. He said that people had come to his house and insisted that he sell them some shells. He did not want to sell the shells but he did because they were so insistent. He evidently felt that he could not frustrate their desires without suffering some consequences, so he gave in to what he considered to be their use of "force."

The next witchcraft incident resulted in the killing of a man (referred to as R) whom I had known over a period of seven years. It was particularly distressing because R was partially responsible for our being given permission to live in San Matías. He argued in favor of us being accepted when others were suspicious of our motives for wanting to live in their village.

This man had advanced through the civil-religious hierarchy until he was elected president. R had served his year as president and was considered to be an elder of the village. We left the village in 1963 and three years later I received a letter stating that this man had been killed. No reason was given for R's murder and when I visited the village a few months later I interviewed five people who were willing to talk about the incident.

The events that led up to his death began when R's mother-in-law's turkey wandered into a neighbor's house. The neighbor's daughter was grinding corn and the turkey began to eat some of the corn. To frighten the turkey, the girl picked up a stick and threw it at the turkey. She not only hit the turkey but killed it and then she was so frightened that she threw the turkey into a ditch without telling anyone about it.

The owner of the turkey came home in the evening and noticed that one of her turkeys was missing. She asked the girl next door if she knew what had happened to her turkey and she replied that she had not seen the turkey. The old woman searched for her turkey until she found it lying in the ditch. She brought it back to her house and accused the girl of killing her turkey. She said that something bad would happen because of this and the girl's father (referred to as L) said that if anything did happen to his daughter he would know who caused it.

It was not long until L's burro died suddenly and his daughter became sick. He went to see the old woman to ask her where she had buried the turkey. She told him and L dug it up to try and call back his daughter's spirit from the turkey. He thought that the turkey had frightened his daughter so that she lost her spirit. But it was too late to help her and she went out of her mind and died. The old woman said that she died because she was the one who had killed her turkey. L blamed her death on the old woman's witchcraft and he went to see the president of the village about the matter. The president told him that there was nothing that he could do since the girl had already died. L next tried to get the alcalde to act but he refused to do anything either except to say that he should be notified if the old woman continued to make witchcraft threats. The whole matter would probably have been dropped then except that L's wife also died.

At this point R made a trip with his wife down to a valley town. It was reported that he went there to ask the resident Catholic priest to say a Mass so that L might be destroyed. The priest was supposed to have agreed to do this and R and his wife returned to the village. When R got back he told a relative of L about the trip. The relative of L immediately passed the word on to him. L then went to the alcalde who had R and his wife arrested.

The alcalde asked a man whose daughter had married a boy from another village to make a trip to that village. He was asked to find out for sure from the people there whether R was practicing witchcraft or not. The people from that town are reputed to be particularly knowledgeable about witchcraft practices. So he made the trip and came back to report that the accusation was true and that L and the rest of his family would all die from witchcraft.

This report convinced the village authorities of R's guilt. He was told to get his witchcraft book so that it could be burned and the matter forgotten. R denied that he had such a book and claimed he never practiced witchcraft. People then began to talk among themselves that they would kill him within a year if he did not give up his practices. He probably recognized the danger he was in so he offered to pay 300 pesos to have the whole incident dropped. The authorities accepted his offer and he then told his wife to pay them the 300 pesos since it was her mother who had started all the trouble.

R's wife raised the money by selling their corn but she said that she was not going to continue living with him. In fact, she began telling people that her husband actually did practice witchcraft. About three months later R and his wife were returning from their ranch to their house in town. It was about midnight when they reached their house and R began to unload his burros. Someone fired at him with a shotgun and the blast caught him in his stomach. He fell dead in the corridor of his house. His wife escaped to another village and has never returned nor probably ever will. The murder was reported to San Carlos but the murderer has never been apprehended although his identity is known to everyone in the village. He left the village immediately after killing R and lives near Salina Cruz.

This witchcraft slaying is typical of others that have taken place in the past in this village and they all include certain shared features. Someone is accused of witchcraft when he makes threatening statements that are believed to cause a victim's death. People can make statements that are considered to be threatening but if no misfortune follows, the threats are soon forgotten. On the other hand, when a person suffers a series of tragedies, he tries to remember who might have made threatening remarks to him. If he cannot remember, he will seek out a curer or diviner to tell him who is the cause of his misfortune.

The reason why people use threatening talk is to coerce others into doing what they want them to do. Thus the old lady who owned the turkey knew that the neighbor's girl would never tell the truth unless she were scared into it. R himself had used threatening talk in the past to scare people for one reason or another. Perhaps his alleged trip to see the priest was his final attempt to convince the village that he was a powerful man who should be left alone. He was unsuccessful both in convincing others of his innocence or of his invulnerability. A few alleged witches have acquired such a reputation for power that some people believe that any attempt to kill them is doomed to fail. Some of the more notorious witches have been killed, not by the act of an individual, but through the concerted action of a whole group of armed men ambushing the witch in his house.

Even when an alleged witch is killed by an individual, the slayer is considered to be acting not as an individual but as a representative of the community. It is necessary then that there be a consensus of opinion that the suspect is a witch before he is killed. Without this consensus, the killer would be subject to arrest by village authorities or revenge slaying by the close relatives of the deceased. This does not mean that everyone will agree that the slain suspect was a witch before or after he is killed. After R was killed, I asked five adult males whether they thought he was actually a witch or not. Three of them believed that he was a witch but the other two did not know. Even of the three who thought that R was a witch, two expressed some doubt. If their opinions are representative of the rest of the villagers, then there was one group of people, with some reservations, who believed that he was a witch and would support community action against him. There was a second group who did not know if he was a witch but would not actively oppose any attempt to kill him. None of the people who were interviewed were related to R but I did have the opportunity to talk to a nephew of the deceased. He did not consider his uncle to be a witch and he told me that if he had been with him the night he was shot, things might have been different.

The village has lost not only R, but his widow and the killer who is afraid to return. The other relatives of the two families involved in the slaying are also living under tension. This was apparent three months after the killing when R's son-in-law made a public demonstration of affection for L. I interpreted this as an attempt by the son-in-law to ward off any suspicion that he was seeking revenge. So it would seem that in the instance cited, the practice of witchcraft raises more problems than it solves. In these mountains, people live under the threat of witchcraft as a type of spiritual blackmail that leads to killings and counterkillings. This climate of fear has caused people to leave the area for their own protection. The population of the neighboring town of Candelaria has been decimated in this way.

Accusations of witchcraft for being wealthy are supposed to minimize the conspicuous show of wealth in a village like San Matías (Wolf 1967:512). The fiesta system could be considered as a wealth-scrambling device that prevents people from getting rich. So, those who become rich through not taking their turn at being mayordomos for fiestas would be subject to envy and witchcraft by their poorer neighbors. The fear of being the object of envy expressed in witchcraft practices or accusations is supposed to cause potential deviants to conform to the expectations of the group. Thus, they will take part in the fiesta system and other economic equalizing devices when they would not otherwise.

The viewpoint just presented is an oversimplification of what happens among the Chontals. Public ridicule alone, without any appeal to witchcraft, is used to prevent some members of the society from deviating. One man, for instance, has held all the offices in the civil–religious hierarchy except president and is old enough to be an elder. But he is not allowed to nominate someone to be mayordomo for a certain fiesta because he has never been mayordomo for that fiesta. He is publicly reminded of that fact and is not allowed to forget it. Still another individual in the village refuses to attend the fiestas and to serve as mayordomo. He has evidently weighed the cost and is prepared to face public ridicule rather than take part in the system.

It is true that wealthy individuals are envied and accused of being in league with the devil. But these accusations do not result in killings. One man who was considered to be rich was accused of being aided by the devil's helpers but he died recently at an advanced age of natural causes. Another man has participated in all the wealth-mixing devices of his society and is still wealthy. He is now being accused of having the same satanic helpers as the man who died. He is aware of these accusations but does not intend to change his way of living because of them. He wants to be different in terms of what money can buy and he is not unduly concerned about witchcraft threats.

There are some good reasons why there are not more witch killings than those that do occur. The religious beliefs of these people make it an unpardonable sin to kill or be killed. Their fatalistic approach to life assigns guilt to both: the murdered one must have deserved his fate because of some wrong that he had done; the murderer by shedding blood for the devil to drink is his agent and shares the devil's fate of eternal damnation. This belief would seem to be such a powerful deterrent against killing witches that one wonders why it is not completely effective. The reason may be that these Indians are more interested in their well-being in the here-and-now than they are in any possible fate in the life to come. An apparent threat to life in this world is evidently far more serious than a possibility of punishment in some future existence.

Another deterrent to killing witches is the belief, mentioned earlier, about the precarious relationship of a person's soul with his body. Any sudden, strong emotion might result in soul loss, sickness, and death. One of R's suspected killers is not a hardened murderer. He is a young man in his twenties who had never killed before and may be affected permanently by this experience. This happened to another murderer of a suspected witch who has since died from what he considered to be the fright that he suffered in slaying his victim.

R's murderer claims he cannot return to San Matías to live because he would be killed by R's relatives. But R's relatives have said that they are willing to let the matter drop so perhaps there is another reason why he does not want to return to the scene of the killing. He may be too frightened to live that close to the dead man's soul. The Chontals believe that the soul of a murdered man is doomed forever to wander in this world near the spot where the killing took place. So the memories that this young man has, plus a respect for the world of the ghosts, may be why he has not returned to his village.

Since witches are killed because they make threats that lead to a victim's death, why would anyone be foolish enough to expose himself by making such a threat? The motivation, as mentioned above, seems to be a desire to gain power and influence over others. And, it is only through the use of verbal threats that the will of the more powerful can be imposed on the less powerful. The risks are great in using threatening talk but the rewards make it worthwhile for some individuals. They possess what can be called negative charisma (Aberle, 1966:226) to an unusual degree. They possess almost unlimited power in the eyes of their villagers because they predict life's most crucial uncertainty, death. Not only do they predict it, but they are believed to actively cause it by magical means that cannot be duplicated by others. Their charisma is negative in the sense that they are disvalued but they are feared to an extent approaching that of supernatural beings. And, in this society as in ours, deviant individuals want to control the lives of others even if it results in the wrong kind of popularity.

Witches exercise their power through the use of the appropriate ritual formula and these ritualistic formulas will be discussed under the section on private religion. Witches, then, do not have any inherent power but are able to affect others through using witchcraft formulas. If a book that appears to be used for witchcraft can be found on the person or in the home of the suspected witch, then that fact is also used to confirm that he is a witch. The question could be asked as to how anyone but a witch could recognize a witchcraft book. The Chontals do not seem to be as concerned with the implications of this dilemma as we are. They try first, as in the case of R, to get him to turn in his witchcraft book. Failing to do that, they take the word of others who claimed that he showed them his witchcraft book. If a search were ever made of the home of a suspected witch, any book of ritualistic formulas that was found could be used as evidence. This would be true because few people can read and of those who can read, few know the difference between religious and witchcraft formulas.

Besides the belief in witches, there is also a related belief in magicians. Magicians, unlike witches, develop inherent power so that they can enter your house, even when it is locked, without bothering to unlock the door. The magician can then steal your property or have intercourse with your wife undetected. There is no actual way to punish a magician since he can break out of jails the same way he enters locked houses. Bullets fired at him have no effect and he has almost supernatural ability to run long distances without getting tired. A man becomes a magician through buying a book of magic in Oaxaca or some other large city and studying it. The apprenticeship is a lengthy one extending up to three years and during that time the apprentice cannot smoke, drink, or have sexual intercourse. The would-be-magician enters into a type of partnership with the devil and the consequences of failing to complete the man's part of the agreement are believed to result in insanity.

A case in point is that of a young man from a neighboring town who was supposed to be studying magic. He arrived in our village one day without his hat, which is rather strange since everyone wears a hat away from home. His speech was disorganized and he did something that I had never seen a Chontal do before—he entered a house without pausing, asking if anyone was home, and waiting for an invitation to enter. There was a woman in the house who hurriedly left as soon as he entered. He left the house as quickly as he had entered and he did not seem to have any purpose in mind in what he was doing. The village authorities called him down to the town hall and questioned him. His answers were so strange that they locked him up in jail and notified the authorities in his village to come and get him. I talked to him when he was in jail and he pointed out to me that the mountain side was covered with people. I looked and could not see anyone. The authorities from his village sent some policemen over to tie a rope around him and take him home. I visited his village later and his father was so concerned about his boy that he asked me if I would look at the books that the boy had been reading. There were some books on magic in among the rest and his father took them and probably destroyed them. The boy recovered from what seemed like temporary insanity and has not had any more attacks. This attack, I was told, was caused by his failure to successfully complete his apprenticeship.

Religion

The religious practices of the Chontals can be divided into two parts: private and public. Perhaps it was always so characterized, but I doubt it. The private religion of the Chontal has probably stayed the same before and after the Spanish Conquest with little or no borrowing involved. The public religion of these people is so Catholic in structure that it is difficult to see any Chontal framework behind it. The two religious aspects, private and public, contrast in as many ways as their names suggest and those differences will be mentioned as each is described.

Private Ritual

There is no aspect of Chontal culture that is as basic to an understanding of that system as the private religion of its individual members. This aspect of their religious life is the last to be shown to foreigners and I am convinced that few outsiders have ever seen it. Many of the Chontals themselves know relatively little about it since it is practiced only by the older adult males. Women are never practitioners of these rituals and young men are for the most part excluded as well. In fact, there is a certain amount of antagonism on the part of the young toward the old people who practice these rituals. This is partially true because the young people do not know enough about the rituals to distinguish religious behavior from witchcraft practices. Then, too, young people tend to be part of the more progressive element of the village that regards these private rituals as superstitious, at best.

The few men who know the correct rituals have a vested interest in keeping that knowledge secret so that they can profit from it. This is another reason why the rites are secret and why misunderstandings can arise. The emphasis of these private rituals is on the letter-perfect performance of them by an individual who is ritually clean. Thus, if the ritual fails to accomplish its stated purpose, the failure can be blamed on the person performing it or the one for whom it was performed. If the performer is to blame, he either was ritually unclean or did not conduct it properly. If the one for whom it was performed is to blame, then he did not remain ritually clean for the specified period of time. In any case of ritual failure, there are always alternative reasons for its failure other than questioning the efficacy of the ritual itself.

A person becomes ritually clean by abstinence from smoking, drinking, and sexual intercourse. He also practices fasting until noon for a specified period of time. The performer of the ritual does not have to practice abstinence or fast for longer than a few days preceding the ritual. The beneficiary of the ritual practices abstinence from smoking, drinking, and eating before noon for a period of from a week to forty days. The president or alcalde must abstain from sexual intercourse for the year that they are in office. This is quite a feat since many of them are in their forties and would otherwise be sexually active. Perhaps this practice is another reason why men offer strenuous objections to serving in the higher offices of the village. The belief that it is dangerous for a man to have intercourse with his wife while he is president of the village persists even among those who reject private rituals. One man told me that he served as president without having the customary private rituals performed but he abstained from having intercourse with his wife during his term of office. He reasoned that whether he believed in the efficacy of the rituals or not was his own personal business but he felt that he had no right to endanger his wife in the process.

Private rituals are performed for every significant event in a Chontal's life that is considered to be dangerous or unpredictable. Thus there are separate rituals for clearing a field for the first planting, sowing the field, and harvesting the crop. Rituals are performed for success in making mescal, bricks, tiles, and lime. And, as mentioned above, there are rituals for all the office holders except the policemen. There is a ritual for digging out a house site and another one for laying the foundation. Birth and marriage also require private rituals. Those who raise livestock have rituals said for their protection from disease and other dangers. Hunters have a ritual to enable them to kill deer who would otherwise be protected by a god of the earth. Villages in the Chontal area differ as to the number of events for which rituals are required, with San Matías being somewhere in the middle.

Each private ritual for the occasions described above is distinctive but they also share common features. They all involve the use of copal resin or sticks that are about as thick as the thumb and a little longer than the middle finger. The sticks are either cut out of the heart of a copal or pine tree and one ritual alone may require over a thousand sticks. The time and patience required for such a task are impressive but the preparations are as secret as the rituals themselves. A man knows exactly how many sticks to cut because he has a little booklet or sheet of paper to follow. (See Carrasco 1960:89, 90 for a reproduction of some pages from such a booklet.) Each appropriate god is offered a row of sticks that have been counted into separate piles. The sticks are laid out at the ritual site which may be the man's field, his house site, the top of a mountain, or a cave. Once the sticks are properly arranged and each god is mentioned by name, the sticks are lit with fire. As they burn, the man performing the ritual may cut off the head of a turkey and throw it on the fire. He picks up the body of the turkey and lets its blood fall on the burning sticks while he names the gods to whom the offering is made. These gods often include the whirlwind, one or more devils, the earthquake, the water, the man of the mountain, the drought, and so on. They even include gods whose names have lost their meanings. He may finish the ritual by burning copal resin in a censer while censing the four directions. If he sacrificed a turkey, he takes it home to his wife to cook.

For three years we lived with a man and his wife who practiced these rituals but kept it secret from us. Once the landlady brought us some turkey broth to eat without letting us know ahead of time that they were going to kill their turkey. This was rather unusual so we asked what had happened to the turkey. She laughed and said that a fox had killed it. It was only much later during our stay in the village that we could appreciate the humor of her reply.

Another time I went with the landlord to his field of corn at the river. The ears of corn were just in the milk stage and he asked me to wait at the edge of the field while he went on a "little errand." When he came back I could smell copal smoke on his clothing but I did not know the significance of it at the time. Later I questioned him about this but he had either forgotten the incident or did not want to remember it.

Actually our daughter was the first one in our family to notice the many sites away from the village where rituals had been performed. She led us to one after another where we could still see the burnt sticks and broken egg shells that remained. When I told the landlord what we had seen, he reluctantly admitted that some people thought they would have better luck in hunting if they performed a ritual first. When I mentioned to the owner of the land that we had seen a number of burning sites on his property, he reacted indignantly and said that he would kill anyone whom he saw performing rituals on his property. Then when I told someone else what the owner of the land had said, he replied that no one but the owner himself would perform rituals on his land.

Once we had discovered something of the extent to which private rituals were practiced, a few individuals were willing to teach us more. They told us about a sacred cave which I later visited. It was near the airstrip, but off the trail and hidden enough so that no one would find it unless he were looking for it. The entrance to the cave was rather small but it opened into a space that was about 5 feet wide by 8 feet long and 6 feet high. The ceiling consisted of huge rocks that had been blackened by the smoke from the copal resin and sticks. On the floor of the cave could be seen the ashes and charred sticks in place from the last ritual performed in the cave. Off to the side was

This ritual arrangement of cut sticks and eggs was "staged" for me by a native curer.

a pile of ashes and burnt sticks from earlier rituals that had taken place at this site.

I was impressed by how much and how recently the cave had been used. No one uses this cave without realizing the seriousness of his action if he should be detected. Once a man related to me that when he was going hunting he saw someone from a distance enter the cave near the airstrip. He waited until the man left the cave and then took a trail to intercept him. When he met the man who had entered the cave, he asked him where he was going. The man gave an indefinite answer and both proceeded on their separate ways. Later the man who had witnessed this told one of his friends in the village about it. His friend immediately asked him why he did not shoot the other man on the spot. Evidently just entering the cave is enough evidence of witch-craft for some people that they would not listen to any other explanations. The man who was detected entering the cave has not as yet been shot as a witch, but he has engaged in activity that might be used as evidence against him some day in the future.

Private rituals are said in Chontal while public rituals use Latin or Spanish. Since devils are included along with the other gods to be appeased in private rituals, there is a tendency for these people to think of them as rituals for the devil. When they have performed or paid to have performed a private ritual, they believe that they have given the devil his due. They give God his due by saying prayers to their household saints or to the saints in the church. Praying or making offerings to both the devil and God is not considered to be contradictory but complementary in the sense that each has been properly remembered. They do not believe that God and the devil are as antagonistic or at such cross-purposes as Americans do in their religious system.

This may be one reason why the Chontals are not as individually con-cerned with sin as we are. They recognize that they are sinners in the sense that they are human beings and as such have a tendency to sin. They accept their sinfulness with the same fatalistic attitude that they have toward their place and position in the world. Because of this diffuse sense of sin, they do not suffer the personal guilt that Americans do. What does concern them individ-ually is their relationship to the gods of this world who can affect their lives through drought, disease, and other misfortunes. Their private rituals function to appease these gods and gain protection from them.

PUBLIC RITUAL

The Catholic friars, in the beginning, and the priests who followed them, have never succeeded in convincing the Chontals that there is only one God. The language barrier has always kept the priest from effectively communicat-ing with these people. It would be easy for him to misjudge their language proficiency because a few individuals will speak Spanish to him. But this Spanish does not include the abstract concepts that are necessary to understand spiritual teaching. The Spanish word *fé* "faith" is not understood by any Chontal that I have asked. And, if they do not understand even the simplest spiritual concepts in Spanish, then anyone trying to teach them religious truths in that language will have discouraging results.

What the Chontal has done is to rename his main deities with Spanish names. The sun was probably the most important god in prehispanic times and since has been named Jesus Christ. The moon also was once a principal god and has since been named the Virgin Mary. An eclipse of the sun or moon is a time of anxiety for a Chontal who believes that death accompanies either event. In the case of an eclipse of the sun, men will die in the village. And, in the event of an eclipse of the moon, women will die. The sun is given the greater reverence of the two; a Chontal man will take off his hat in respect as he sees the sunrise.

A Chontal believes in the effectiveness of using a surrogate to approach anyone from whom a request is asked. This is true not only of a boy asking his father to talk to a girl's parents for him, but the father may also feel that he would get better results if he used a go-between. The surrogate is usually someone who knows both parties and can use his influence to help the one asking the request. The same principle is carried over to their religion by having lesser deities as surrogates. A person presents his request to them with the belief that they in turn will intercede to God on his behalf. The Chontal has reason to believe in his lesser deities being alive and capable of relaying his requests. So, even though the priest may tell him that the saints are men whom he should honor, but not worship or pray to, it would probably not be accepted.

The priest is the most important person in the public ritual of the Chontals. No priests live in the highland area, but one lives in Tequisistlán and another in Huamelula. Between the two of them they visit all the mountain villages for a day or two at least once a year. Their visit is a time for couples to be married in the church and for the baptism of babies. Both priests are American and are attempting to deemphasize the importance of fiestas and to emphasize the more spiritual aspects of the Church. So, to the disappointment of the villagers, the priests refuse to make their visits during village fiestas. I have heard people from several villages make the statement that they would rather not have the priest come at all if he will not come for the fiesta of their patron saint. Neither priest has made a serious attempt to learn the language of these mountain people, so all communication is in Spanish with the inherent problems mentioned above. After the priest conducts Mass, he often preaches a sermon to the people which, from the later versions that I have heard, is seriously distorted in the process. There is no use made of the confessional and people resist attempts to have them pay any tithe offering beyond the cost of the ceremonies of marriage and baptism. The priest only charges a nominal fee for each of these ceremonies, but it is insinuated that he makes a great deal of money in this way. When no priest is present, one or two village cantors, accompanied by the village band, sing the Mass for Sunday services, fiestas, and funerals.

$$\boxed{4}$$

Personality System

T HERE ARE DIFFERENT VIEWS held by anthropologists about what a description of personality ought to include in a study of a group of people. One view is that such a description should deal only with individuals and their histories whether they are representative of the group or not. In this view any statements made by the anthropologist apply only to the individuals involved and are not meant to be applied to the entire group. It is felt that once statements or generalizations are made about the personality of a group, the anthropologist is no longer talking about personality but is dealing with culture.

Another view is that individuals are only of interest to anthropologists as they are representative of a group of people. The emphasis in this approach is on the effect that social and cultural systems have on psychological development and consequently on the distribution of personality characteristics in the group or community. This effect can be detected in the art, literature, and religion of the people. Both of the above viewpoints will be developed, but the emphasis will be on the second.

Individual Personality

A Chontal is not accustomed to giving long accounts about his life. The main reason why the two individual accounts that follow are presented here is because we were able to find two people who were willing to talk at some length about themselves. In each case the English translation follows closely what was said in Chontal so that distortion is kept to a minimum. The first text was transcribed as it was dictated to my wife by the woman involved. The second text was transcribed from a tape recording that I made of a conversation with the subject.

I consider the woman in the first account to be more acculturated to the Mexican culture than most Chontal women. She speaks better Spanish than they do and has had her hair waved. She is in her late twenties or early thirties and prefers dresses to the native costume. The following text describes her courtship:

When I was twelve years old I was making tortillas in our kitchen. It was late afternoon. X came and stood outside the door. The door was partially closed because it was windy and I didn't want dust in my tortillas. He called and asked if someone was home. When I answered, he asked if we had any pig fat to sell since we had killed a pig the day before. (The question was asked by my wife, "Did you know X before this?") Yes, he used to come by to play with my older brother but I didn't pay any attention to him because I was too shy. I didn't think about getting married. I wanted to grow up first. Anyway, X stood around for a long time and then he finally left. Some time later I was alone again, making tortillas, when X's father came by. He said, 'Is your mother here?'

I said, 'No.'

'When will she be back?'

'I don't know. Maybe today or tomorrow.'

'Well, tell me when.'

'Well, I don't know.'

'Okay, I'll come another time.'

The next day he came again and the conversation was the same. I told my grandmother and she said, 'What could he want?' The next day my mother came home. She just got home and right away X's father and mother came. He said his son wanted to marry her daughter. Well, my mother said that we'd have to think about it and give the answer the next Saturday. She had to know what I thought about it. I said I didn't want to get married—I wanted to stay with my mother until I was older. But my mother said, 'Go ahead and marry him. I have too many children to feed and clothe and I don't have any money.'

Well, the next Saturday they came again, the two, and my mother went into the house to talk to them. I hadn't agreed to marry him. I stayed in the kitchen. I heard her tell them that I would marry X and I hadn't even said I would. Then X's father asked the name of my padrino so he could go see him. And he had to go to San Miguel since he lived there. So he went and right away he said that I would marry X. Right away my mother gave me away and I hadn't agreed to it. Well, they gave the dowry and four weeks later he took me.

(Question: During those four weeks did you talk together?) Well, right away after he gave the dowry, whenever my mother was away, I always went off to my grandmother's. I didn't want to stay there alone. I'd stay with her all day.

(Question: Did he help you?) Yes, he'd help my brothers. He'd work with them in our fields and they would work with him. And after work he'd come right to our house to be fed. He wanted me to feed him and my mother said I should but I didn't want to. I didn't want him with my whole heart.

One afternoon I was all alone and he came. He said he was hungry. He wanted me to feed him. I told him there wasn't anything. He said he knew there was. After a while when I wouldn't give him anything, he left.

Another time I was at my grandmother's. It was getting dark so I started to leave. I told my grandmother that my brothers, sisters, and I were going home to sleep. She said, 'Go ahead.' So we left. I heard him call me. He was hidden. I got scared. It was dark, and I was alone. What could I do? When we got to my house he came right in with us. He said he was going to sleep there. We were going to sleep together. I said we couldn't do that. He insisted. I said my grandmother might come but I just told him that to get rid of him. Still he insisted. So I said, 'Well, if you're going to sleep here you can sleep in that bed over there. I'll sleep here with my brothers and sisters.' But he insisted he was going to sleep in bed with me. I was ashamed because of my brothers and sisters being there. Finally he left. Oh, I got so happy then.

This marriage has been a childless and generally unhappy one. The woman has never enjoyed intercourse with her husband and still experiences pain when they copulate. He has been unfaithful to her in the past and they have had bitter quarrels, accusations, and innuendos. She has also had constant mother-in-law conflicts that have eased up some since they have moved to their own house.

She impresses me today as being neurotic and constantly complaining about vague symptoms and chronic ailments that are not susceptible to the kind of medical treatment that she can afford. Most of her problems, real or imaginary, would probably be solved if she could only bear children. She has been pregnant only once to my knowledge and it ended in a miscarriage. Her husband has grounds for leaving her because of her childlessness; he has threatened to do this a number of times in the past. He seems now to be reconciled to the situation and the issue, though present, is not the source of contention that it used to be. Other women tease her about her small breasts because they have never been enlarged with milk.

She is not representative of other women in that she was not eager to marry at an early age. Also, her situation was different in that her widowed mother forced her to marry because of economic problems.

The second account is of a young man twenty-five years of age who describes his religious conversion. The questions that appear in the text were asked by me to either clarify a point or encourage him to keep talking. The text is as follows:

Well, first I thought carefully, worked hard, and made some money.
And how did you make this money?
I made it by selling chickens and eggs down in Tehuantepec.
And how much do you buy a chicken for here?
Here you can buy them for 8 or 10 pesos.
And how much can you sell them for there?
You can get about 12 or 15 pesos for them there.
And eggs?
You can buy them here for 30 centavos and you can sell them there for 50 centavos. That's what I did, and when I had made about 400 pesos, then I bought a female burro.
Did you buy it here or in some other village?
I bought it in San Lorenzo.
How much did you pay for it?
Three hundred and twenty-five pesos.
Was it fully grown?
It was pregnant when I bought it. Then I bought a small male burro for 150 pesos. I wondered about the ritual customs and what I could do so that my burros wouldn't die. Since I made trips, I always brought back candles to burn

and, sometimes on Sunday, I would read a prayer. I would pray to God that he
would help me so that my animals wouldn't die.

Did you do this in church?

No, I did it in my house. Once in a while I'd go to the church.

Did you pray in Spanish or in Chontal?

I prayed in Spanish.

Then there is a prayer for that?

That's right. There are all kinds of prayers for that. There is a prayer, *Dios
Padre* or *Padre Nuestro,* whatever prayer that you want. And so I prayed with all
my heart because they said that was the right thing to do. And, daily I burned a
candle. Then I asked about the ritual customs and had them performed for my
animals.

Did you pay someone to do this for you?

Yes, I did. I bought the ritual formula and my dad performed it. I paid 15
pesos for the formula and then we fasted while we were performing the ritual. . . .

How many days did you fast?

Nine days.

What was it like?

We fasted until noon every day and then placed our candle. We had carried
out the custom.

Where did you perform it?

In a ravine where I have a piece of ground.

Isn't there any particular place where you have to carry it out?

No, so long as it's your own ground. But, you don't want to do it on someone
else's ground because they might get mad about it. Six months after we had
performed the customs, I got up early one morning to look for my female
burro. I couldn't find her anywhere. She had gotten loose by herself and had
wandered off. Then I heard an animal down below making a sound like a hog.
The animal was running and I thought it must be one of my hogs.

When I got down to where the animal was, I saw it was my burro, laid out
with her stomach all swollen up. When my dad saw the burro, he said right
away that someone caused her to get sick.

And how was it done?

Someone looked at her. Right away we rubbed her body with an egg all over
and my dad took it and left it some place. When the sun had risen to about
noon, my burro was dead.

What good does it do to take the egg and leave it some place?

They say that then the sickness will leave. After she died, I did a lot of thinking. I wondered why this had happened to me. I had done everything I was
supposed to do. Then a friend of mine had gone to Mexico City and had found
out about another religion. He gave me some tracts to read and taught me how
to sing some hymns. But I didn't want to follow this new religion. I didn't
know whether there was anything to it or not. I felt that I couldn't follow it
because I still had animals and I was afraid that they might die. I was accustomed to burning candles but after my burro died I began to have doubts.
Maybe there wasn't anything to our customs. Then about three days later I tied
my little burro to a tree and when I got up early the next morning he was dead.
He had choked himself on his lasso and when I saw him the rope was around
his neck and passed over his stomach between his legs. I had tied this burro up
before so he knew what it was to be tied. As soon as I saw how he had died I
realized that this had been done by the devil. The devil himself had choked my
burro. Now both of my burros were dead. As soon as that happened to me I
stopped doing the customs. I stopped going to church. I stopped burning
candles. I stopped saying the prayers. I saw that the whole thing was false. I
had tried it. I did what you were supposed to do and it didn't work. To this

day I haven't done any more customs. Instead, I follow this other religion. We still get sick but now we treat ourselves with medicine and we always get well.

I've done the things that they say you can't do without performing the customs. For example, I was secretary of the town and I didn't perform any rituals before I took office. And I got married without the ritual custom. I didn't have anyone say a formula or perform a sacrifice for me. Children have been born to me and I haven't performed the customs. I built a sugar cane press without customs. I plant beans and I don't do any customs. The only thing I do is pray to God. I pray every day and hope that my relatives as well will change their ways because what the old people have told us is not true.

This young man belongs to a Protestant group in San Matías that numbers less than a dozen converts. It has been functioning for about six years without any new members being added. As a member of such a small group he is not representative of most of the young men in the village. His attitude toward his old religion, though, may be quite similar to that of many young people who have left the highland area and no longer follow Chontal customs.

Typical Psychological Characteristics

The balance of this chapter will deal with the relationships between socialization, psychological characteristics, and other social institutions.

SOCIALIZATION IN THE FAMILY

The extended family that the child is raised in has been discussed in the chapter on the Social System. The child is nursed either until another sibling is born or until he is between two and three years of age. One reason for this lengthy period of nursing is that there are no baby foods available that would ease the transition from milk to solid food. Cooked corn atole is the only food that even approximates what a baby needs in this transitional period. Often he is fed other foods that result in indigestion, worm infestation, and diarrhea that can be a serious threat to his life. The breast is also used as a pacifier to keep the child from crying. The weaning of children among the Chontals, as compared to our society, is characterized by a long period of initial satisfaction with a great deal of permissiveness. The same can be said to characterize his toilet training which has also been discussed under the Social System.

His sexual training seems permissive to me. The baby is in close body contact with his mother not only in nursing, but whenever she or one of his siblings carries him. He is often naked and seldom fully clothed until after he has been toilet trained. It is permissible for boys up to four years of age to be dressed in only a shirt, which does not cover their sex organs. Girls' dresses are not soiled as easily as boys' pants and they wear dresses at an earlier age. Little boys and girls play together quite freely until the girls reach nine or ten years of age. One incident of sex play that I know of occurred near our former landlord's house. A little girl of about six or seven years of age was playing with a boy of about the same age on the main trail through the village. In the presence of adults, she lay down on her back and pulled her dress up. This exposed her sex organs and she told the little boy to climb on top of her. Some of the adults saw what she had done and laughed at the incident. They did not get upset about it or report it to her mother.

With this early sexual permissiveness it would seem that the adolescent and adult Chontal would have a more relaxed attitude toward sex than Americans do. But the opposite is true. I have never seen a married couple display affection for each other in public. My wife observed an engaged couple once from a distance. They were alone. They talked with their backs to each other and never touched one another. But the incident that I remember most vividly occurred on one of my weekly mail trips. As I was walking through Candelaria, a young man stopped me. He wanted some kind of medicine but he was so uncomfortable and embarrassed that I could not understand him. Finally, little by little, he told me what he wanted. His wife, who must have been in her teens, was frigid and he wanted medicine that would make her more passionate. His problem was revealing of his attitude toward sex in that he thought that medicine would correct what was probably due to his own inadequate sexual technique. However, he was so concerned about the problem that he was willing to talk to a stranger even though he suffered acute discomfort.

One possible explanation for the inhibitions that these people have about sex may be due to their sleeping arrangement. The whole family, which may include older married siblings and their spouses, sleep together in one room on bamboo beds. Under these circumstances, a young married woman may be so concerned about being detected in the sex act that she may not be able to have an orgasm. Also, children raised under such an arrangement are almost certain to hear their parents in the act of copulation. If this takes place when the child is very young, he would not understand the significance of the act, and the noises could frighten him. If he was alarmed in this way at a pre-language age, there would be no verbal way of comforting him. On the other hand, if the detection took place after he could use language it would be unlikely that his parents would give him a clear explanation for an act about which they are ambivalent.

A fourth system of behavior, dependency training, is also contrastive with our American culture. The long period of nursing and permissiveness in toilet training may encourage dependency, given the context of social relations that exist in later years. Children are not taught to compete with each other to the extent that they are in our culture. Nor is there the competition between parents to push their children into walking and talking at an early age. Dependency is also encouraged by the size of the extended family in which the child is raised. Decisions are made by the older members of the family without consulting the younger members. The father is much more of an authoritarian figure in the Chontal family than in our culture and even an adolescent boy nearing twenty is reluctant to make an independent decision. A young man once came to me with a serious eye injury. I could see that a thorn was lodged in his eyeball near the pupil and I tried to impress upon him the need to go immediately to a doctor in Mitla and have it removed. I offered to pay his way if he would leave immediately but he kept insisting that he could not make the trip without his father. His father was on a trip himself at the time and would not be back for several days to a week. By the time his father did return, the urgency of the situation had passed and nothing has ever been done to his eye.

The last behavior system to be discussed here is aggression. Chontal parents are both permissive and strict in dealing with the aggressive behavior of their children. They are permissive in their handling of temper tantrums in that they try to avoid them by giving in to the child's demands. They believe that any strong emotion is dangerous for the child to experience because of the possibility of soul loss. Consequently some parents will not force their children to do something if the child strenuously objects. Once a mother brought her sick baby to our house for medicine. He began to cry as soon as we gave him the medicine. She told an older child who came along with her to run home and get some water. She filled her mouth with the water and sprayed it out in a fine mist in a semicircle on the floor of our house. As she did this, she called to the spirit of the baby, using the baby's name, while she took her shawl and swept the baby's soul back into his body. She got up and left our house with her children without offering any explanation for what we thought was the strangest Chontal behavior we had ever witnessed.

On another occasion a woman asked me, while I was talking to several men in our house, if she could scrape some of the dirt off our walls. I said that she could but I wondered why she would want to do that. She explained that I had given her boy some medicine in the past in our house and she thought that maybe he had been frightened since he was still sick. She believed that he had lost some of his soul to the walls of our house. After scraping off a little dirt from the adobe wall, she mixed it with water and had her boy drink it. The other adults watched this with me without expressing any disapproval.

Small children are not disciplined for hitting their parents but they are stopped from fighting with their siblings. I never saw an actual fight between children during our stay in San Matías. As soon as one child hits another, a grown-up steps in and punishes the aggressor.

PSYCHOLOGICAL CHARACTERISTICS

The adult Chontal is generous with what he has and this trait has definite survival value for these people whose subsistence base is often precarious. Every time that I have called at a man's house while he was eating, he has asked me to eat with him. Before I am allowed to leave a house where I am visiting, the owner insists that I take along some fruit to eat. Once a man gave me a young chicken as a gift for visiting him—a gift worth a day's wages. Because he is generous, the Chontal does not accumulate material wealth to any extent to pass on to others. This means that each generation starts off fairly equal in terms of inherited wealth.

The Chontal is even-tempered. The ideal man never loses his temper even when he has been drinking. We lived in a separate room in the house of the landlord and his wife for about three years. Not once did we ever hear them quarreling with each other, nor did we ever hear them verbally fighting with other people. One of the worst things that can be said about an adult is that he has a hot temper that he does not control. Fighting is considered to be a serious offense that is dealt with by the village authorities to restore the kind of harmony that a face-to-face society requires.

An adult is suspicious of others and what they can do to him through witchcraft. This may be caused or aggravated by the suppression of aggressive behavior in children. But it involves more than just suppression. The Chontal's world view is such that he personalizes what are impersonal forces to us. Sickness is thought of as a person who comes and goes and has supposedly been seen in the shape of an old woman. Desires are considered to be so powerful that they press for realization and often cannot be denied. I have tried to reason with individuals about the impossibility of anyone causing them harm through jealousy or witchcraft but my explanations have not satisfied them. Once a man from another village came to me for medical treatment because he had inhaled poisonous fumes. His throat had been burned but otherwise he was not physically affected. He was so emotionally upset, though, that I had a difficult time trying to reassure him that he would recover. I treated him with medicine for a while but he refused to stay in San Matías. He claimed that the woman who was cooking his tortillas was trying to use witchcraft on him. He claimed that he could actually feel her evil power radiating out from the cloth in which she wrapped his tortillas. He would not (or could not) eat her food and he told me that she would kill him through witchcraft if he did not leave the village. He went to the nearby town of Candelaria and took my treatment there until he felt that he had recovered.

A Chontal is group-oriented rather than individualistic. He feels more satisfied if a decision has been made by the whole group of which he is a member rather than by a few individuals in authority. This is why the elected officials never make any important decisions without the elders being present to give their opinions. If it is a major problem under consideration, the elders want all of the men of the village present for moral support, if for no other reason. I noticed that even the most talkative and influential elder in the village becomes uncomfortable if others do not express their opinions also. He once said that he was going to stop talking so much because others would blame him for any mistakes made by the village.

These mountain people do not impress me as being as competitive as Americans. I mentioned earlier how even in as competitive a situation as a basketball game a tie is accepted as a satisfactory conclusion. A major concern of many people is to avoid calling attention to themselves in any way. They do not want to be considered either poor or rich but somewhere unnoticed in-between these two extremes.

They lack confidence and self-esteem, but it is difficult to determine whether this is due to child training practices or to their position in the larger Mexican society. Mexican society has little racial prejudice but it does practice class prejudice. Painful encounters with prejudiced Mexicans, such as those mentioned earlier, may be the reason why Chontals lack self-esteem. They realize that they are superior to Mexicans in being able to work longer and harder, but inferior because they cannot participate adequately in the Mexican culture.

The psychology of a Chontal seems much like that of the Pueblo Indians described by Benedict as Apollonian (Benedict 1934). Both have the same measured approach to life and stay within the common traditions of their people. Neither meddles with disruptive psychological states and both distrust any form of individualism. This distrust of individualism is so strong among the Chontals that any social deviant is a potential object of witchcraft accusations. Even the practitioners of private ritual, especially those who are recognized as being more knowledgeable, do not stress their personal qualifications. Instead, they sell a written ritual that is supposed to be effective because it tells how to perform the appropriate ceremony in letter-perfect detail.

FOLKLORE AND PSYCHOLOGY

Religion and folklore may be considered as ways of looking at the world in terms of a society's conflicts. Since religion has already been discussed in some length, this section will deal only with folklore.

The folklore of the Chontals can be classified into five main themes or motifs: odd man, trickster, superman, cheater, and good man. The odd man theme is illustrated by a folktale called Juan Ceniza, or John Ashes. This tale, like almost all other tales told by the Chontals, did not originate with them. They borrowed them from sources that would be impossible to trace today. The source of the tale is unimportant. What is important is that of all the tales that they have heard, these particular tales appeal to them. They have modified them so that the tales are even more interesting to them and these modifications are in turn of interest to an anthropologist. The tale of John Ashes consists solely of an account of a man who refused to live in a house like ordinary people, but preferred to live in an ash heap. In spite of the pleas of his family and friends, and even though they would force him to come into the house:

> ... after he had eaten, after they fed him, he would run away to the ash pile and lie in it.
> Then when it was clear that this was his way of life, they said to him, 'Why do you lie in the ashes? Why do you live in the ashes? Is that better? Or is that where your house is?'
> He replied, 'I just like it. This is my place. I've gotten accustomed to it, lying in these ashes. Day and night I am here. This is where I live. This is my place.'

The above story strikes people from our culture as being no story at all in that it has a weak plot and an unsatisfactory ending. But this story is both humorous and appealing to the Chontals. The basis for its appeal may be due to the stresses that they experience living in a face-to-face society. Everyone knows everyone else and lives in what impresses us as a fish-bowl existence. No matter how hard he tries, the Chontal has difficulty maintaining any kind of private life. If he does decide to act contrary to group norms, very real pressures are brought to bear on him to make him conform. These pressures take the form of ridicule by the village for relatively minor infractions. For the more serious deviancies, there is always the threat of being called a witch or being the object of witchcraft. The village authorities also step in with fines, imprisonments, beatings, and hard labor for anyone who violates specific social norms.

The popularity of this story seems to indicate a deep, unexpressed desire on the part of Chontals to take part in deviant behavior. They would prefer not always to have to conform, but to do as they please without group pressure. This is not a possibility for them in everyday living because they have to conform in countless ways. So they enjoy telling a story about someone who does what he wants to do no matter what others think.

The second theme of Chontal folktales is the trickster theme. There are more stories expressing this theme than any other and this suggests that it is the most important of all themes to the Chontal. One such story involves a turtle and a lion. The lion had decided that he was going to eat the turtle but each time they met, the lion was outsmarted by the turtle's trickery and deceit. Finally, the lion found the turtle as he was cracking nuts. He told the lion that they were delicious and gave him one to eat. The lion ate it but said that he was still going to eat the turtle. The turtle argued that the lion was not going to eat him but instead he was going to eat some nuts. He told the lion that the way to eat nuts was to take his testicles and put them on a rock. Then he was to take another rock and crack his testicles so that he could get at the nuts. The lion did what the turtle suggested and killed himself.

This story has the theme of an "underdog" winning out over his more powerful foe through devious means. The tale has a great deal of appeal to the Chontals and one reason may be that they consider themselves inferior to more knowledgeable outsiders. They identify, I think, with the trickster because they would like to compete successfully against the more powerful Mexican. Their encounters with him, though, tend to have the opposite result so that only in their folktales does the disadvantaged one consistently win.

A third theme of Chontal folktales is called the superman theme. This theme is illustrated by the story of a boy who was born to a woman in a cave. No mention is made of the father of the boy but the setting is such that it can be inferred that a god of the earth copulated with the woman. The boy grew up to be so strong that he was called Fourteen Strengths. But he did not know his own strength and constantly caused his godfather, who was a priest, one problem after another. The priest tried to have the boy killed but he won out in tests of strength with the devil and all his helpers, a tiger, and twenty-five soldiers. When the priest gave up trying to kill the boy he gave him a machete with which to build a house. The machete was so big and heavy that no one else could lift it. Fourteen Strengths built his house and when his time came he died a natural death.

At first glance this folktale ends in an anticlimatic way. Yet, it may be building up to what is important to a Chontal—the inevitability of fate. If Fourteen Strengths himself was subject to fate in spite of his superhuman strength, how can a mortal man fight and win against it? A Chontal does not fight against what he considers to be fate but cooperates with it and bows to what he interprets as an irresistible force. This type of resignation may help the Chontal to accept with patience what we consider to be a life of abject poverty. Unfortunately, at times his fatalistic attitude results in his not trying to change certain areas of his life that could be better controlled.

A fourth theme in the folktales of these mountain people is the cheater theme. These stories deal with marriage infidelity, always focusing on the woman's fault in the act. One story describes how a man who suspected his wife of being unfaithful spied on her from a tree. He saw her and another man attempt to have intercourse while they neighed and acted like horses. The husband returned home undetected and told his wife at the supper table that they should both neigh like horses. She was so startled by this request that she eventually died from fright. This pleased her husband because she took her own life without him having to do anything.

From this story and others there seems to be an underlying anxiety experienced by Chontal men about marriage fidelity. This may be due to two factors: a kinship system that has already been described which severely limits the number of eligible mates for a male; and, the high rate of women's deaths in childbirth. Since a man's eligible mates are reduced to the point where he may find it difficult to find a wife, he is concerned about the factors that could take his wife away. Adultery on the part of his wife is one of these factors. In each of these stories dealing with unfaithful wives, the wife is always punished in some extreme form while the same is not true of her partner in adultery. The other factor, death in childbirth, is a too-common occurrence. The term used for a woman's death in childbirth is the same one used for a man taking a woman to be his wife. This suggests that Chontals regard death in childbirth as a result of someone, baby or spirit-being, taking away a man's wife.

The fifth and last theme to be discussed is the good man theme. This theme is illustrated in the story of a man who asked Saint Anthony for success in making money. The saint agreed to this request, and in return, the man was to be generous to his fellow men. But he soon forgot this part of the agreement and became stingy. Saint Anthony heard about it and disguised himself as an old man. He asked the rich man for some food, and was not only refused, but verbally abused as well. So Saint Anthony withdrew his blessing from the rich man and the man lost all he owned.

This story helps to explain the extreme reluctance of a Chontal to refuse a request for food. We never saw our landlady turn anyone away who was hungry or implied that they wanted her to give them some food. People will not ask to be given food that they want but will instead offer to buy some. Since small quantities of food or mescal are not sold, this is a more polite way of requesting a gift. Once the landlord and I raised some onions and we split up the crop later on our porch. People saw us putting onions into bunches and later came by to "buy" some. They were given onions by the landlady for nothing but none of them had any success in persuading us to "sell" them our part of the onions. This was partly due to our misinterpretation of their use of the word "sell." We needed the onions more than the money that they would sell for because our nearest supply source was Oaxaca City, about seventy-five air miles away. Also, we were either more stingy with what we owned than our partners or we did not have the same cultural compunctions to share what we had.

I am not qualified to psychoanalyze these two people with whom we shared a house and say which behavior was purely unselfish and which was motivated by a guilty conscience. Time after time we were impressed with their generosity. As time passed we developed an extensive medical work and people came to us from a distance of up to a day away over mountain trails. Sometimes their treatment required that they stay over for as long as two weeks. But it was the landlord and his wife who moved out of their house and allowed sick ones to sleep there while they slept on the dirt floor of their lean-to kitchen. Often he shared his food with these strangers without assurance of being paid back.

This kind of situation where a good man is generous caused us real conflict. We had so much more to be generous with and yet we believed that our own health required that we maintain a certain standard of living. Our own cultural values of the worth of personal property and the dignity of providing for your own needs inhibited us from following the Chontal pattern.

In this section I have, for the most part, tried to show how the social and cultural systems of the Chontals affect their psychology. Our daughter, who was only six years old when we began to live in San Matías, was also affected. She played with the children in the village for most of every day during the four years that we lived there. We did not realize how much like a Chontal child she was becoming until an incident occurred that was reported to us by an antimalarial sprayer. He was from Oaxaca and knew us from his earlier trips to San Matías. He told us how on this occasion he happened to come upon some children in the village while they were playing. He surprised them and they reacted in typical Chontal fashion by running away from him. Our daughter was playing with them and she also ran from the outsider. He was hurt enough by her behavior to come and tell us about it and we began to recognize how effective the social and cultural systems of the Chontals were, even to the point of affecting so decisively the behavior of our own child.

5

Cultural Change

THIS DESCRIPTION of the Chontals thus far has emphasized the uniformity and static characteristics of their society. Actually their society, like all other societies, is constantly changing. This implies that there are important differences between individuals as well as internal dissatisfactions in the society. This chapter will emphasize the internal dissatisfactions experienced by the Chontals as they are part of the larger, more powerful Mexican society. There are factors that set limits on the amount of change that can take place in response to these pressures and they will also be discussed.

Internal Dissatisfactions

The dissatisfactions that the Chontals experience are for the most part due to their interactions with the Mexican society. This society has an admirable lack of racial prejudice based on physical characteristics. It is, however, a stratified society that discriminates against people on the basis of social class. The lowest class in the society is the poor and uneducated Indian who is made to feel inferior in all of his dealings with the Mexican.

The Indian is poor because the land he is trying to farm is marginal land. This land in many instances is only suitable for growing lumber or grazing stock and is damaged by attempts to raise food crops on it. The food that he grows cannot be sold because its yield is too small to produce a surplus. He is poor because he is uneducated and unskilled in any type of business or industrial trade. When he works for someone else, it is always doing manual labor that pays the lowest wage. This wage is so low that it is difficult, if not impossible, for him to save any money after paying for his living expenses. Any money that he does save is for immediate goals and not for the accumulation of business capital. The kind of a society with which he has his first allegiance disvalues the long term saving of money that the Mexican society values. He is supposed to be generous and share what he has with his relatives and friends. He takes part in the wealth-leveling fiesta system and serves without pay in all the offices of the village. His own society discourages him from getting an adequate education or training. The language spoken in his home is either Chontal or an impoverished type of Spanish. Neither language provides a suitable base for the teacher to build upon—the teacher speaks only Spanish. Instead, much of his time is spent in teaching what amounts to a new language to children who never hear it spoken except in school or over the radio. A young man would have to leave his village after the few years of substandard schooling that are offered to go live in a lowland city if he wanted to compete in the Mexican society. This requires an amount of money that his parents would be unlikely to have and an adjustment that would be difficult for him to make in a strange city.

The Mexican society emphasizes the importance of competition and individual achievement. The Chontal is poorly prepared by his culture to participate in an achievement-oriented society since his own culture stresses opposite values. He is raised in a social system that gives prestige to its members on the basis of sex and age and deemphasizes individual accomplishments. The old and conservative male of the Chontals is respected in his society because of who he is. This contrasts sharply with the ambitious and mobile young man of the Mexican society who is admired for his accomplishments.

Point by point, as discussed above and throughout this book, the Chontal culture is at cross purposes with the Mexican culture. The Chontals are part of a minority culture that functions poorly in terms of preparing them to participate in the majority culture. Unfortunately the Chontal has tended to accept the Mexican's opinion of him, his language, and his culture. The majority culture exerts pressure on the Chontals to change and their response is limited by the multiple factors already mentioned: poverty, lack of communication, and cultural values.

Attempts at Cultural Change

The issue could be raised as to why anyone has the right to attempt to change another person's culture. Somehow we believe that this is even a more serious issue when the people involved are from different cultures. So a teacher of anthropology may be openly critical of a missionary or culture change agent because he is trying to change people's beliefs and practices. But the teacher never seems to view his own role as that of a cultural change agent actively persuading students to accept biological evolution as a fact and to practice cultural relativity. He believes that criticism of other cultures is evidence of ethnocentrism and critical statements should be recognized as biased statements. But the same individual will criticize his own society for its shortcomings and not recognize his statements as being biased. There seems to be a double standard here and, whether we like it or not, cultural change is almost inevitable when people interact over an extended period of time. The rest of this chapter describes my attempts at changing the Chontals' culture to one more like my own.

SUCCESSFUL ATTEMPT

The acceptance by the Chontals of "modern" medicine can be considered an example of cultural change in an additive rather than a replacive sense. That is, "modern" medicine never replaced all of their folk medicine but each was considered effective for different sicknesses. I have called the kind of medicine and medical practice that we introduced "modern" only in the sense that it contrasts with their folk medicine.

We had some practical training in medicine before we arrived in the village and we brought with us some medical supplies. We intended to use this medicine mostly for ourselves because we had no way of anticipating how many people would want our medicine. The first medicine that I can remember selling was to a woman who had a bad toothache. Her relatives had asked me if I had any medicine to help her and I gave her some pills for her pain and packed her tooth with cotton dipped in oil of cloves. It was effective and people began coming to me for medicine from all over the village.

Word spread to other villages that I not only treated the sick but charged reasonable prices that they could afford. I had dramatic effects treating a young man from Zapotitlán who went back to his village and told his friends and relatives about his cure from what he thought was a serious ailment. About half of all the people I treated from that time on were from his village. Our medical practice reached over a hundred cases a month with patients coming from almost every Chontal village. They came for medicine, minor surgery, or to have teeth pulled.

When we realized that we would have to leave the village, I began to train a young man to continue the medical practice that I had started. I taught him how to give a local anesthetic before pulling a tooth. I showed him how to give a sterile injection of vitamins or penicillin and what symptoms called for each type of injection. We went over the symptoms of the diseases that were most prevalent in the area and he wrote down the proper medicine and dosage for each of these. He has been more successful pulling teeth than in practicing medicine, but he has done both. People are gradually gaining confidence in his ability and go to him for help when I am not in the village. He is honest, sincere, and is trying to do a good job of treating people at reasonable prices.

In many respects I consider the medical practices that we introduced to be the most satisfying part of living with these people. An anthropologist has to find a suitable role to play other than writing an ethnography if he lives with a group of people who do not understand what anthropologists do. This is important not only because of what they think about him but also because of his own self-image. Practicing medicine gave me a sense of doing something worthwhile. I felt, as they did also, that I was a productive member of their society. I did not raise corn or distill mescal like every other male in the community did but I was available for medical emergencies and other treatment throughout the day or night. At times when certain factions in the village wanted the rest of the people to tell us to leave, I suspect that my value as a doctor of sorts was all that persuaded them to allow us to stay. They never understood the reasons that I gave for wanting to live with them but they did appreciate having someone in the village who could help them medically.

There were several reasons for our success in introducing modern medicine. The superiority of modern over folk medicine was readily apparent to them. None of their folk medicines could relieve pain or lower a fever or stop diarrhea as effectively as our medicines could. And even more important, none of their medicines could inhibit the spread of disease or kill the offending organisms. None of their curers could remove objects that had entered their bodies. Instead, they came to me when they had been shot to have the bullet removed. When their ears were plugged up with wax they came to me to have the hard wax washed out.

Their folk remedies were ineffective for stopping the pain of a tooth-ache and their method for extracting teeth was too painful for most people to use. In the past they had knocked out the offending tooth by placing the point of a stick against it and hitting the other end of the stick with a rock. This may be effective at times but the pain is too much for most people to bear. I was surprised to discover that in spite of their almost stoic approach to life, these people could not stand pain any better, if as well, as we. I made the standing offer to pull anyone's tooth for nothing if he could take the pain without the use of a local anesthetic. Out of perhaps hundreds of patients, I can only remember two people who ever allowed me to pull their teeth without first using an anesthetic. In both instances the teeth to be pulled were so loose that I was able to convince them that there would be almost no pain.

Modern medicine was also far superior to their folk medicine because they only had remedies for a few ailments and even then there was no con-sensus about their effectiveness. One man told me that a skin rash on your feet could be cured by walking on tomatoes that were tied around your feet with bandages. But even though his treatment actually is effective in helping some skin rashes because of the acidity of the tomatoes, he, typically I think, ex-pressed his own doubts as to whether it was worth trying.

Modern medical treatment proved to be less expensive than their folk treatment so this was another reason why they accepted it. They could often be treated for a few pesos' expense or less when they came to me for medicine. But the old curer began his charges at this level and went up to 25 pesos or more. He often was not able to help them, nor was I, and if they continued looking for a folk treatment, they had to go to someone in a lowland village. These curers were very expensive, charging up to 300 pesos for their treat-ments which did not involve the use of medicines. They were psychological treatments at best and ineffective against organic disorders.

Disease or a disabling accident produces a great deal of anxiety in a folk society. This is due in part to their past experiences with relatives or friends dying after a brief illness. Sickness or accident also produces anxiety because of the low subsistence level of these people. There is not enough of a surplus for anyone to be a noncontributor. He becomes a burden very quickly and senses this keenly. In addition there is no appropriate role for him to play as a sick or disabled man in his society. He has no doctor to put him under "doctor's orders" not to work, so his disability lacks some of the credibility that it would have in our society. There is no hospital to go to and be with other sick people, but instead he is somewhat of an oddity as the only sick person in an otherwise healthy family.

A disability is especially a matter of concern to a Chontal because much of his public and private ritual is intended to protect him from such an event. He has been raised to believe that if he is faithful in offering each god what has been prescribed in his ritual formulas, then no evil will happen to him. A disability is the worst evil that could occur, with the exception of death, and he wonders why it should happen to him. An explanation that would satisfy us in terms of exposure to germs, or an accident being due to carelessness, is not an acceptable explanation to him. He views the world as being alive in a sense that we do not and the only satisfying answers to him are those that are in terms of personal forces. He believes that if he gets hit on the head by a dislodged rock from above while he is hoeing in his cornfield, and no human agent is present, then the field is angry with him and has not been properly placated.

Sickness is more difficult to assign a cause to than is an accident, which occurs in a specific location and involves a definite agent. When a Chontal becomes sick he has to classify the disease as a good disease or a bad one. Good diseases come from God and are sent to cause people to suffer for their wrongs. This type of sickness may affect a whole village, and, if it does, this is an indication that the disease is from God. Diseases that God sends are susceptible to treatment, so if a person takes medicine and recovers, then he knows that God sent the disease. This is an incentive to take medicine as the first step in getting well and also as a means of determining the source of his sickness. Once he recovers after a treatment with medicine, he is satisfied as to what caused his illness and looks no further for an explanation. This conclusion was the right one as far as I was concerned because it reduced tension in the village.

Unsuccessful Attempt

This attempt at culture change involved the language and religion of the Chontals. My family and I went to live in San Matías as linguistic missionaries serving with an interdenominational Protestant missionary group. Our task was both secular and sacred. We planned on making a linguistic analysis of the Chontal language and publishing our results in scientific journals, and we succeeded in doing that. This analysis was then to be used to help us reach another secular goal: to increase the degree of literacy among the Chontals. We felt that this goal could be realized best by teaching the Chontals to read their own language first and then using that knowledge to help them in reading Spanish. We failed in doing that because we were never able to interest them in reading their own language. The religious part of our task was to translate portions of the Bible into their language. In order to do that we had to learn their culture as well as their language. There were no Protestants in San Matías when we arrived in 1959 but there was a group of Jehovah's Witnesses in the neighboring village of Zapotitlán. This group had been active for fifteen years and had succeeded in converting perhaps half of their village. No one in San Matías or in any other village had been converted to this doctrine even though this group of Jehovah's Witnesses had been actively seeking converts. The only other contact the villagers of San Matías had with Protestants was when a small airplane had dropped portions of the Bible in Spanish from the air about ten years before our arrival. Some people in the village had picked up the booklets and saved them although they could not understand the level of Spanish used.

We were recognized immediately as being Protestants because we had no saints in our house, but people were willing to overlook this peculiarity since we did not try to convert them. After we had lived in the village for several years we began to translate the Gospel of Mark into Chontal. This involved working with language helpers so that our mistakes would be corrected and the translation would sound as natural as possible. In the process, a half dozen men heard the Gospel of Mark in their own language for the first time but showed no interest in asking any questions about it.

One woman who had lived for a few months in the lowland village of Salina Cruz did become interested in becoming a Protestant after helping my wife translate portions of the Bible into Chontal. Her husband, X, did not share her interest but came along at times to help also. We took this young couple with us to a translation conference held near Mexico City in the fall of 1962. They lived with us there for two months and helped us in our translation work. X was impressed with the number of Protestants that he saw and lived with, but showed no interest in changing his religion. He liked the hymns he heard and enrolled in a Bible correspondence course through a Mexican friend that he met.

He and his wife returned to their village of San Matías several months ahead of us with what seemed to be the same attitudes that they had when they left us. His wife was still interested in Protestantism, but he was, if anything, even less interested. We were surprised when we returned to the village to hear that he had been teaching hymns to his friends and relatives. We suggested that they meet in our house each Sunday and we would teach them more hymns and discuss a portion from the Bible. We had our own house at this time, which we had built the year before. It was our own idea to move out of the landlord's house since, even though he was still friendly, he had no interest or sympathy with Protestantism. We had a large room that the people could meet in, but so many came that there was not enough room for everyone. After this initial show of interest, the group leveled off to about thirty-five people who came each week. The group, though, only included about a dozen adults and the rest were teenagers or younger. X succeeded in enrolling about twenty people in the Bible correspondence courses. These people were all in their twenties or younger but none of them understood enough Spanish to answer the questions. I helped as many as I could with their lessons and the rest copied from them. About eight people completed the course and received their framed certificates.

We left on a one year's furlough in August of that year and we allowed the group to continue having their meetings in our home. After we had been gone for a few months, someone threw gravel on the metal roof of our house while the group was having a meeting inside. This, along with other threatening behavior scared them so much that they decided to give up the meetings for awhile.

When we returned for the summer in 1964, only eight people were interested in meeting together in our home. They continued to meet each Sunday, even after we left at the end of the summer. A Pentecostal church in a lowland village heard about these Protestants in San Matías and sent a preacher to instruct them. The preacher was an aggressive evangelist who held meetings in our house every night. The village authorities reacted to his evangelistic attempts by jailing him and X for three days. As soon as the authorities released them, the preacher and X went to the district head of San Carlos and returned with a statement from the judge. The judge's statement was delivered to the village authorities. It said that they had no legal right to imprison anyone because of his religion. They were told not to interfere with the religious practices of the Protestants who were free to practice their own religious beliefs.

This statement ended all attempts by the village authorities to harass the Protestants or to compel them to take part in activities associated with the religion of the village. But the Protestant group did not grow, even though their situation was somewhat eased. The Pentecostal preacher returned with another evangelist for a series of meetings but their excessive emotionalism and attitude against medicine repelled the Chontals. The Protestant group is now functioning on its own, but instead of growing in numbers, it is losing members one by one. Some are leaving the group to return to the religion of the village. Others are leaving or thinking of leaving the area to live somewhere else.

This attempt to introduce Protestantism has, to put it mildly, met resistance and been unsuccessful. Resistance is a symptom of something wrong in culture change and I will try to identify what went wrong. Of course it could be argued that religion is one of the greatest resisters of change and I should not have expected any success. But the Jehovah's Witnesses in the neighboring village of Zapotitlán have succeeded in introducing Chontals to a type of Protestantism so that this argument is not as convincing as it first sounds.

First, the people of San Matías had no desire to become Protestants. They had been exposed to the evangelizing attempts of the Jehovah's Witnesses and they consistently rejected their teachings. Nor was there any pressure to follow the lead of other towns since Zapotitlán was the only Chontal village to have any Protestants. Actually, San Matías was a poor choice in which to begin any attempt at changing its religion or that of the area. The attempt should have been made in a more prestigious village such as Ecatepec or San

Miguel because any success experienced in those towns would have influenced San Matías.

One reason why Protestantism met resistance is that the older people in the community saw it as a threat to their status. If they accepted Protestant doctrine they would have had to admit that they had been wrong and the wisdom of their years and that of their ancestors was therefore not to be trusted. This is extremely difficult for an elderly person to do because he has believed for so long that it is a part of his identity. To change his beliefs he must also change his identity and that is particularly painful for an aged person. He had waited patiently for the years to give him the status that old people enjoy. He would lose status by becoming a despised Protestant and would have to interact in a different religious system. He would be unsure of his role in this different religion where the ability to read the Bible and sing hymns seemed to be so important. This new religion called attention to his inadequacies in the same way that contact with Mexican culture did and he found the prospect unpleasant. How could he join a group whose leader was a much younger man than he? His society had always stressed the importance of age and he found it difficult, if not impossible, to respect a man who was so much younger than he.

Another reason why Protestantism was rejected by most of the village is that it seemed to be incompatible with their fiestas. Since the fiestas of the village were in honor of the saints, a Protestant could not take part in them. He believed that there was only one God and because of religious belief he could not be mayordomo for a fiesta. But every adult male is supposed to serve as mayordomo and if he does not he will be accused of disloyalty to the village. Since a Protestant cannot serve as mayordomo, he could be ridiculed if he ate at the mayordomo's house. He could not in good conscience attend Mass or dance or drink anymore—his only forms of recreation.

Still another reason why Protestantism was rejected is because it did not seem to have any status or support in the larger Mexican culture. The more knowledgeable Chontals know that Catholicism is practiced from the capital of Mexico down to their village level. But they had never heard of Protestantism or had been confused by its fragmentative appearance of denominations and cults. Protestantism, as introduced to San Matías, seemed to be the religion of an American who came from a quite distinct and different culture. His religion appeared to be suitable for him and his family but unacceptable for a Mexican Indian.

Effects on Me

Perhaps I should have discussed the successful attempt at culture change after the unsuccessful one to have a more satisfying ending to this book. I chose the other order of presentation because it is my own impression that I did very little to change the culture of the Chontals in any fundamental way. Sometimes they accepted something from me without my even being aware of trying to change them. This is even more true of their effect upon me. They did not consciously try to change my way of life but they did, and in a more pervasive way than I had affected them. This is ironic in that culture change agents are constantly warned about the seriousness of attempting to change someone else's culture but are not told about how their own lives may be affected.

One basic purpose I had in mind in going to live among the Chontals was to change their religion. But the result of living with them for four years was that my own religious views were changed. I had accepted the doctrine that all people who did not accept the Gospel message would be eternally damned. I had no difficulty believing this until I got to know several Chontals in a personal way. Then one of these individuals, an elderly lady who reminded me of my own grandmother, died before I was able to communicate the Gospel to her in her own language. As I stood at her newly dug grave and watched her body being lowered into the ground, the unfairness of it all struck me with such force that I could no longer believe in a doctrine that would damn her.

I went to the Chontals assuming that a sense of personal guilt for sin was a cultural universal. As soon as I had learned their language well enough to discuss such topics, I began to talk to them about sin. Once I tried to convince a man that he was a sinner because he must have committed at least one of a list of sins that I mentioned. He listened to my attempt to convince him of personal sin and replied, "You know, there are people here like that." He missed the personal application completely as did every Chontal with whom I talked. It affected me profoundly to realize that they were not concerned with personal sin and that I had a solution to something that they did not consider to be a problem.

The culture of the Chontals contrasted in so many essentials with our own culture that I was able for the first time to look objectively at our culture. I had gone to the Chontals as a participant–observer of their culture but returned an observer of our culture as well as the participant that I had always been.

References

ABERLE, DAVID F., 1966, "Religio–Magical Phenomena and Power, Prediction, and Control," *Southwestern Journal of Anthropology,* Vol. 22, pp. 221–230.

BENEDICT, RUTH, 1934, *Patterns of Culture.* Boston and New York: Houghton Mifflin.

CARRASCO, PEDRO, 1960, "Pagan Rituals and Beliefs Among the Chontal Indians of Oaxaca, Mexico," *Anthropological Records,* 20:3. Berkeley and Los Angeles: University of California Press.

WALLACE, ANTHONY F. C., AND JOHN ATKINS, 1960, "The Meaning of Kinship Terms," *American Anthropologist,* Vol. 62, pp. 58–80.

WOLF, ERIC R., 1967, "Types of Latin American Peasantry," in *Tribal and Peasant Economies,* George Dalton, ed. Garden City: The Natural History Press.

Recommended Reading

GOODENOUGH, WARD H., 1963, *Cooperation in Change,* New York: Russell Sage Foundation. This book stresses the various aspects of agent–client cooperation that are necessary for successful culture change.

NASH, MANNING, 1966, *Primitive and Peasant Economic Systems,* San Francisco: Chandler Publishing Company. The author deals with the dynamics of social and economic change from the viewpoint of an economic anthropologist.

REDFIELD, ROBERT, 1960, *The Little Community* and *Peasant Society and Culture.* Chicago: University of Chicago Press. These two books appearing under one cover emphasize the relationships that a peasant society has to the larger society in which it must function.

SCHUSKY, ERNEST, AND T. PATRICK CULBERT, 1967, *Introducing Culture,* Englewood Cliffs, N.J.: Prentice-Hall, Inc. A basic introduction to the concept of culture without technical jargon.

TAX, SOL, AND OTHERS, 1952, *Heritage of Conquest: The Ethnology of Middle America.* Glencoe, Ill.: The Free Press. Specialists from both North and Middle America discuss aspects of culture of the people of Middle America.

WHITING, JOHN W., AND IRVIN L. CHILD, 1953, *Child Training and Personality: A Cross-Cultural Study,* New Haven: Yale University Press. The authors describe the effect of childhood training on a typical personality in a number of societies.